Practical AutoCAD®

Randall McMullan

BLACKWELL SCIENTIFIC PUBLICATIONS

OXFORD LONDON EDINBURGH

BOSTON MELBOURNE

© 1989 by Randall McMullan

Blackwell Scientific Publications
Editorial offices:
Osney Mead, Oxford OX2 0EL
   (*Orders*: Tel: 0865 240201)
8 John Street, London WC1N 2ES
23 Ainslie Place, Edinburgh EH3 6AJ
3 Cambridge Center, Suite 208
   Cambridge, Massachusetts 02142, USA
107 Barry Street, Carlton
   Victoria 3053, Australia

First published 1989

Typeset by DP Photosetting, Aylesbury,
Buckinghamshire
Printed and bound in Great Britain by
Mackays of Chatham PLC, Chatham, Kent

DISTRIBUTORS
Marston Book Services Ltd
PO Box 87
Oxford OX2 0DT
(*Orders*: Tel: 0865 791155
         Fax: 0865 791927
         Telex: 837515)

USA
Publishers' Business Services
PO Box 447
Brookline Village
Massachusetts 02147
(*Orders*: Tel: (617) 524–7678)

Canada
Oxford University Press
70 Wynford Drive
Don Mills
Ontario M3C 1J9
(*Orders*: Tel: (416) 441-2941)

Australia
Blackwell Scientific Publications
(Australia) Pty Ltd
107 Barry Street
Carlton, Victoria 3053
(*Orders*: Tel: (03) 347-0300)

British Library
Cataloguing in Publication Data
McMullan, R. (Randall)
   Practical AutoCAD.
   1. Design. Applications of microcomputer
   systems. Software packages: AutoCAD
   I. Title
   745.4′028′55369

   ISBN 0–632–02486–0

Library of Congress
Cataloguing-in-Publication Data
McMullan, Randall.
   Practical AutoCAD/Randall
   McMullan.
      p.   cm.
   Includes index.
   ISBN 0–632–02486–0
   1. AutoCAD (Computer program)
   I. Title.
   T385.M394   1989
   620′.00425′02855369—dc20

Trademarks mentioned in this book belong, as indicated, to the following
organisations:

Autodesk Ltd: *AutoCAD, AutoSolid, AutoCAD AEC*;
Epson Corporation: *Epson*;
Hewlett-Packard Company: *Hewlett-Packard*;
IBM Corporation: *PC, PC-DOS, PS/2*;
Microsoft Inc.: *MS-DOS, OS/2*;
AT&T Bell: *UNIX*

Contents

Introduction

AutoCAD has established a world-wide standard for computer-aided drawing and design, especially for users of microcomputers. The program has evolved with the power of these machines but anyone who knew AutoCAD almost 10 years ago would still be able to 'drive it'. Meanwhile, the 'wishlists' of users are constantly being fulfilled so that AutoCAD and its associated packages can carry out the CAD tasks needed by current practice.

The very power of AutoCAD creates an initial problem of use. Any device that does complex tasks under your control requires some learning – there is no such thing as 'simple-to-learn' jet airliner controls! The use of such controls, however, can be made as efficient as possible.

You don't have to know all of AutoCAD's features to get productive results and, unlike flying an aircraft, there are no physical dangers. Sections of this book are therefore focused on the practical *procedures* for creating drawings with CAD packages. During my years of learning about CAD, this has always been the hardest type of information to find. Mainly, I think, because the procedures are new and flexible.

The text and structure of the book tries to provide help at relevant times and purposely avoids the sheer weight of some trans-Atlantic books on AutoCAD. Having sat with dozens of people learning AutoCAD I know you that you will learn to draw a rectangle, say, in a very short time and do *not* need that particular operation accompanied by 10 pages of text and diagrams!

CAD gives you freedom to break old rules, to reach the same final drawing on paper by many different methods and, above all, to change your mind. The very opposite of the old-style draughting texts, not to mention instructors, who were so *rigid* about what to do. Nevertheless, some CAD procedures are more efficient than others and I hope that this book gives you ideas that can be refined for your own applications.

My thanks to everyone who has helped in the preparation of the book, especially to Autodesk, the proprietors of AutoCAD, who are always so helpful.

Randall McMullan

Using This Book

Part One of the book contains summaries of the main groups of AutoCAD features and commands. These self-contained Prompt Pages use few words but they should be enough to start you on a new area of commands or to remind you of forgotten ones.

Part Two of the book shows AutoCAD in actions with a series of practical examples which lead from the simplest shapes to complex drawings. The examples contain keyboard instructions and also demonstrate the various good practices of CAD which can be so different to hand-draughting.

Part Three is an AutoCAD information section which gives more information about advanced features and summaries of the commands and variables. There is also information about versions, installation and customisation of the program.

Remember to watch the screen while you use AutoCAD and to read the prompt line. The program itself is often asking you a question or providing you with the information that you need. Experiment and practise while on screen. This is often faster and more effective than dozens of words and it doesn't do any harm. It may even change your life!

Part One
AutoCAD at a Glance

EQUIPMENT

Computer: The AutoCAD program benefits from running on a 'fast' type of computer because drawing is one activity where the speed of the computer system produces noticeable effects on screen.

AutoCAD also needs the speed and large storage capacity of a hard disk. Modern versions of AutoCAD require that the *maths co-processor* chip is installed in appropriate microcomputers.

Screen: The AutoCAD program works by mathematical methods so its accuracy and its appearance on paper do *not* depend on the screen display. There are several standards of display to choose from, depending on your needs and on your budget. The options involve the size of the monitor screen, the resolution (fineness) of detail, and the colour abilities.

AutoCAD can be set up to work with all graphics standards and may also drive two screen displays, one for drawing and one for text information.

Keyboard: The keyboard of a microcomputer or terminal contains the alphabet keys, as on a typewriter, which can be used to give AutoCAD commands.

- The RETURN key, which may be labelled ↵, or 'Enter' is used to conclude a keyboard entry.
- The space bar, at the bottom of the screen, is also used for some AutoCAD operations.
- The extra function keys found on many computers, labelled F1, F2 etc., are used by AutoCAD as shortcuts for some settings.

Mouse: The mouse is one type of pointing device used to move the AutoCAD crosshairs around the drawing screen and over lists of command words. To *pick* a point on the drawing, or to choose from a list, one of the mouse buttons is pressed. Another button on the mouse will also act like the RETURN key.

Digitiser tablet: A digitiser is an electronic board over which a *stylus* or *puck* is moved like a pen, causing the AutoCAD crosshairs to move around the screen. A plastic sheet or *template*, containing AutoCAD commands, can be placed on the digitiser and calibrated to the program. Commands can then be given by pointing while drawing.

Plotter/printer: A *pen plotter* uses moving pens to produce a paper copy of an AutoCAD drawing. Plotters are available for different sizes of paper from A4 to A0.

A *printer plotter* is a printer which can use its graphics ability to produce AutoCAD drawings. Most dot-matrix and laser printers allow this.

EQUIPMENT

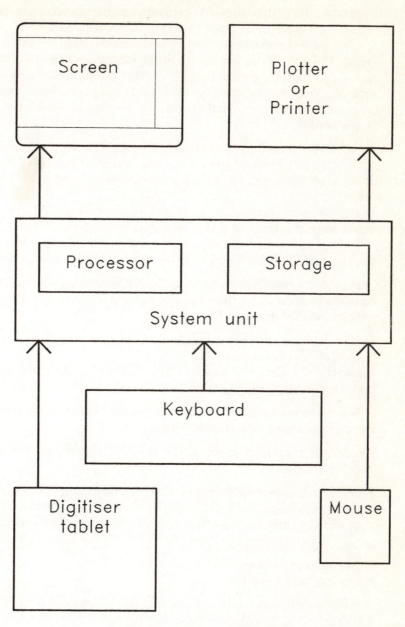

Components of a CAD system.

STARTING

It is assumed that the AutoCAD program files are already installed on your computer. If necessary, see Part Three of the book for information.

After the computer has started up you should use the operating system, such as PC-DOS, MS-DOS, OS/2, to log onto the disk drive and the directory which contains the AutoCAD files. Then enter *acad* to start the program. You can also use an interface, such as Windows, to start the AutoCAD program. Once started, the AutoCAD program provides its own environment of displays and methods, which are the topics of this book.

AutoCAD program: The *Main Menu* of AutoCAD is a text screen which lists the various parts of the program and gives you access to them. From this screen you can choose to draw, to set up AutoCAD to suit your equipment, and to keep your drawing files in order.

The *Drawing Editor*, or graphical part of AutoCAD, is the main working environment for creating and editing drawings.

To start any section of the program just type the number listed on the Main Menu and press [RETURN]. Use Ctrl-C to cancel a wrong command and start again.

Starting a drawing: When you select the NEW drawing option AutoCAD asks you to enter the filename of the drawing. The method of entering this filename also affects the settings used for drawing. For example:

house   The new drawing called 'house' will start with the standard settings of your version of AutoCAD.
house=style1   The new drawing called 'house' will start with the settings saved in a prototype drawing called 'style1'.

When you have entered the filename, AutoCAD loads the drawing editor and puts the monitor screen into graphics display.

Finishing a drawing: Use the END or QUIT command. See the Prompt Page on 'Storing' for details.

Filenames: A drawing is stored on disk as a collection of electronic information kept together in a 'file'. Each drawing file must have a distinct 'filename' supplied by yourself. The main rules for filenames on microcomputer systems are:

- Alphabet and numbers only.
- Maximum of 8 characters.
- No spaces or full stops.

A system of prefixes can be used to refer to a file stored on another drive or directory. For example: *b:\work\plan1* refers to a file called *plan1* which is located on drive B in the directory called *work*.

STARTING

OPERATING SYSTEM
Typical commands
to load AutoCAD

```
C:\>CD\ACAD

C:\ACAD>ACAD
```

AUTOCAD
Main menu

```
Main Menu

    0.  Exit AutoCAD
    1.  Begin a NEW drawing
    2.  Edit an EXISTING drawing
    3.  Plot a drawing
    4.  Printer Plot a drawing

    5.  Configure AutoCAD
    6.  File Utilities
    7.  Compile shape/font description file
    8.  Convert old drawing file
```

AUTOCAD
File menu

```
File Utility Menu

    0.  Exit File Utility Menu
    1.  List Drawing files
    2.  List user specified files
    3.  Delete files
    4.  Rename files
    5.  Copy file
```

AUTOCAD
Setup menu

```
Configuration menu

    0.  Exit to Main Menu
    1.  Show current configuration
    2.  Allow I/O port configuration

    3.  Configure video display
    4.  Configure digitizer
    5.  Configure plotter
    6.  Configure printer plotter
    7.  Configure system console
    8.  Configure operating parameters
```

COMMANDS

AutoCAD is made to work by giving 'commands'. The special command words feature in all AutoCAD operations, and throughout this book. When AutoCAD is ready to receive a command, the line at the bottom of the screen shows the following 'prompt' –

Command:

A command can be started by a choice of methods, described below. Always read the prompt line to check the next input needed by AutoCAD.

Most commands have *options* or *subcommands* to choose from. The <brackets> show the default setting – just press [RETURN] if you are happy with the default shown in the brackets.

Keyboard: A command is started by typing the command name, with careful spelling, and then pressing [RETURN] or the space bar.

Screen menu: The commands are listed in groups (submenus) on the screen to the right of the drawing area and written as follows.

● UPPER CASE letters are used for command words.
● Lower case letters are used for subcommands or options.
● An apostrophe (') indicates a *transparent* command which can be used inside an existing command.

A command is activated by moving the crosshairs onto the command word and pressing the pick button of the mouse or other pointing device. The cursor keys can also be used to move the crosshairs. If no command is chosen then the crosshairs can be moved back onto the drawing area of the screen.

Tablet menu: Commands symbols are given an area of the digitising tablet during setup. A command is then started by pointing the stylus or puck to its command symbol and then pressing the pick button.

Pull-down menus: An additional menu bar appears along the very the top of the screen in most versions of AutoCAD. Selecting a menu title with a pointing device causes an appropriate choice of commands to drop down.

Dialogue boxes: The pull-down menus also allow you to change settings by using the pointer to indicate choices on special graphic displays. You must confirm some settings by pointing and picking an 'OK' box.

Function keys: AutoCAD runs on many types of computer but it is common to use a keyboard with function keys, labelled F1, F2 etc., which can quickly change useful settings as Grid and Snap.

Repeated commands: The previous command can be reissued quickly by pressing the [RETURN] key or the space bar.

COMMANDS

Screen menus

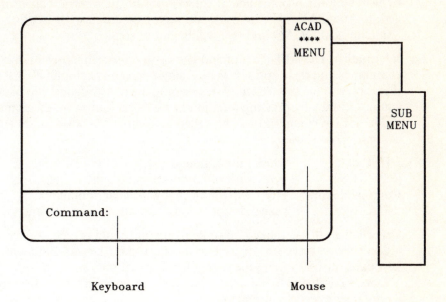

Keyboard   Mouse

Pull-down menus

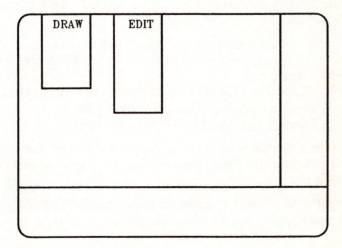

HELP

AutoCAD can give you help information about the meaning of commands and also give you help routines to recover from mistakes. You can help yourself to a large extent by watching the prompt line at the bottom of the screen. This prompt shows what action AutoCAD expects next and takes precedence over other menu displays. Sometimes AutoCAD and you will be out of step!

Information: The HELP command gives you on-screen information about AutoCAD commands and their options. With a single-screen system the HELP command 'flips' the display to the text screen. After reading the text you must flip back to the drawing editor – usually by pressing function key F1 or a button on the pointing device.

The HELP command can be called in a variety of ways, and can be used after a command has started.

HELP or ?   starts the command.
[RETURN]   gives a list of commands and general help.
Command name   gives help about that particular command.
'Help or '?   suspends operation of another command and gives help.

Cancellation: If you make a mistake then you should reverse sooner rather than later – don't try to drive out of it! Use the backspace key to erase simple errors at the keyboard, such as typing the wrong letter for an option.

Once a command has started – watch the prompt line to confirm this – you can use the following cancellation methods.

Ctrl-C   (hold down the Ctrl key and press C).
Screen menu   (move the cursor and pick 'AutoCAD' at the top).
Tablet menu   (pick the 'Cancel' area of the tablet).

UNDO: The UNDO command has various options which retrace a sequence of commands and undo their effects, one by one:

Number   x. Enters the number of commands to step back.
Auto   A. Groups any item into a single command which can be reversed
             by a single U.
Mark   M. Places a marker in the undo information for the Back option.
Back   B. Performs UNDO effects back to previous Mark.
Control   C. Disables or limits the UNDO command.

U: The U command undoes the most recent AutoCAD operation and is equivalent to the UNDO 1 command. The U command can be repeated and works backs one command at a time.

REDO: The REDO command undoes the effect of an UNDO or U command. It must be entered immediately after the command.

HELP

HELP command – typical screens

```
   AutoCAD Command List   (+n = ADE-n feature, ' = transparent command
APERTURE +2    BREAK +1      DIM/DIM1 +1    END            HIDE +3
ARC            CHAMFER +1    DIST           ERASE          ID
AREA           CHANGE        DIVIDE +3      EXPLODE +3     IGESIN +3
ARRAY          CIRCLE        DONUT +3       EXTEND +3      IGESOUT +3
ATTDEF +2      COLOR         DOUGHNUT +3    FILES          INSERT
ATTDISP +2     COPY          DRAGMODE +2    FILL           ISOPLANE +2
ATTEDIT +2     DBLIST        DTEXT +3       FILLET +1      LAYER
ATTEXT +2      DDATTE +3     DXBIN +3       FILMROLL +3    LIMITS
AXIS +1        'DDEMODES +3  DXFIN +3       'GRAPHSCR      LINE
BASE           'DDLMODES +3  DXFOUT         GRID           LINETYPE
BLIPMODE       'DDRMODES +3  ELEV +3        HATCH +1       LIST
BLOCK          DELAY         ELLIPSE +3     'HELP / '?     LOAD

Press RETURN for further help.
```

```
   AutoCAD Command List   (+n = ADE-n feature, ' = transparent command)
LTSCALE        PEDIT +3      REGENAUTO      SNAP           UNDO
MEASURE +3     PLINE +3      RENAME         SOLID          UNITS +1
MENU           PLOT          'RESUME        STATUS         'VIEW +2
MINSERT        POINT         ROTATE +3      STRETCH +3     VIEWRES
MIRROR +2      POLYGON +3    RSCRIPT        STYLE          VPOINT +3
MOVE           PRPLOT        SAVE           TABLET         VSLIDE
MSLIDE +2      PURGE         SCALE +3       TEXT           WBLOCK
MULTIPLE       QTEXT         SCRIPT         'TEXTSCR       'ZOOM
OFFSET +3      QUIT          SELECT         TIME           3DFACE +3
OOPS           REDEFINE +3   'SETVAR        TRACE          3DLINE +3
ORTHO          REDO          SHAPE          TRIM +3
OSNAP +2       'REDRAW       SHELL/SH +3    U
'PAN           REGEN         SKETCH +1      UNDEFINE +3
```

```
If  REDO  is entered immediately after a command that undoes something
(U, UNDO Back, or UNDO nnn), it will undo the Undo.  An UNDO after the
REDO will redo the original Undo.

See also:   Section 5.5 of the Reference Manual.

Command:
```

STORING

Leaving a drawing: Do *not* switch off your computer with a drawing still on the screen. AutoCAD needs to close its various files and to store your work on disk, otherwise you might lose your drawing and leave spurious files. The following commands are used to leave the drawing editor:

END   Returns to the Main Menu and saves the current state of the drawing in the drawing file. The old copy of the drawing file becomes the backup, and any previous backup copy is deleted.

QUIT   Returns to the Main Menu but does not save any drawing or changes you have made. You must also confirm Y(es) or N(o) to leaving the drawing.

SAVE   Saves the current state the drawing but remains in the drawing editor to allow further work. The old copy of the drawing file becomes the backup file.

Drawing files: A drawing is stored on disk as a collection of electronic information kept together in a 'file'. Each drawing file must have a distinct 'filename' supplied by yourself. The main rules for filenames on microcomputers are:

- Alphabet and numbers only.
- Maximum of eight characters.
- No spaces or full-stops.

When storing a file AutoCAD adds a suffix of three letters which are separated from your 8-character filename by a dot. The suffix *.dwg* indicates the current drawing file, and *.bak* indicates the backup file. AutoCAD uses other suffixes such as *.sld* for slide files, *.dxf* for drawing interchange files.

A system of prefixes can be used to refer to a file stored on another drive or directory. For example: *b:\work\plan1* refers to a file called *plan1* which is located on drive B in the directory called *work*.

If you are using an operating system other than MS-DOS, PC-DOS, OS/2 it is useful to restrict yourself to simple filename rules as it helps the exchange of drawings between systems.

File maintenance: The File Utility option of the Main Menu allows you to list, delete, rename and copy files. You can also use the operating system to do the same 'housekeeping'.

STORING

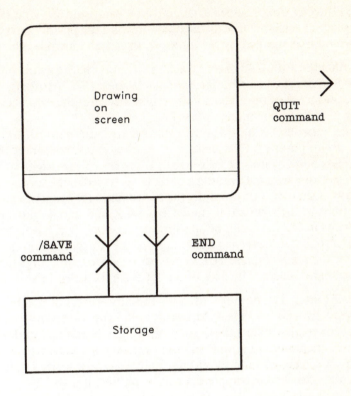

Typical file list

```
File Utility Menu

    0.   Exit File Utility Menu
    1.   List Drawing files
    2.   List user specified files
    3.   Delete files
    4.   Rename files
    5.   Copy file

Enter selection (0 to 5) <0>: 1

Enter drive or directory: A:

AIRPLANE.DWG   CHAIR-3D.DWG   CHROMA.DWG   COLUMBIA.DWG
MPART-3D.DWG   NOZZLE.DWG     POINTS.DWG   STAIR.DWG
9 files
Press RETURN to continue:
```

DRAWING SCREEN

The Drawing Editor screen is where you create and view your drawings. The *cursor* is the place in screen where the next action will take place. For drawing operations, the active point is marked by the intersection of two movable crosshairs.

Coordinates: AutoCAD keeps track of any point in a drawing by a system of Cartesian coordinates called the *World Coordinate System* (WCS), usually shown by a symbol at the bottom left of the screen. This system measures the distances of the point from the 'origin' in fixed directions or 'axes'.

The horizontal X-axis is given x numbers and the vertical Y-axis is given y numbers. The *origin* point (0, 0) is usually at the lower left corner of the drawing. Negative numbers allow you to go below and to the left of the origin.

In two-dimensional drafting a point is expressed in the form (x, y) with the x distance always given first. For example, the coordinates (5, 4) specify a point which is located at 5 units to the right along the horizontal X-axis and 4 units up the vertical Y-axis.

Points in 3D space can be specified by using (x, y, z,) coordinates where the Z-axis projects out of the screen at right angles to the XY plane. You can also define your own *User Coordinate System* (UCS) whose origin can be anywhere within the World Coordinate System. The axes of the UCS can be tilted in any convenient direction.

Drawing units: The numbers used for the coordinates of points also give the distances between two points. These 'drawing units' can represent metres, millimetres, feet, inches or whatever suits the current drawing. Coordinates and units can be entered as decimal fractions and AutoCAD itself maintains numbers to a precision of at least 14 digits. A screen drawing should normally use the full-sized units of the actual object. When the drawing is complete it can be plotted at a variety of scales on paper.

Drawing boundaries: AutoCAD has various terms for different drawing and viewing areas. These rectangular areas are specified by the coordinates of the lower left corner and the upper right corner:

- *Drawing Limits* are the borders of the current drawing rectangle. The drawings limits specify the potential size of your drawing, but they are not restrictive and you can draw outside them.
- *Drawing Extents* are the borders that just fit around all objects drawn so far.

Screen display: Your monitor screen acts like a window through which you can see all or part of a drawing. The screen display can be moved about over the drawing by *panning*. The drawing seen on display can also be magnified or reduced by *zooming*.

- *Display Extents* are the borders of the current screen display.

DRAWING SCREEN

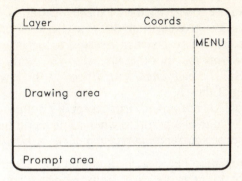

Drawing screen areas

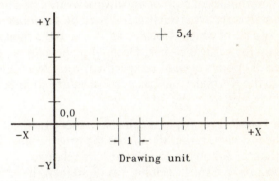

Coordinate system

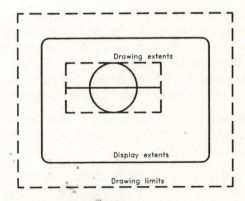

Drawing boundaries

LOCATIONS

The AutoCAD program keeps track of every point in a drawing by a coordinate system which you can use to specify the accurate location of objects. The coordinate system can also be used to give accurate distances between points.

Point coordinates are given in relation to origin of the *User Coordinate System* (USC). Unless you specify otherwise, the USC is the same as the *World Coordinate System* (WCS). The *coordinate system icon* at the lower left of the screen shows the current setting of the UCS.

Many AutoCAD commands can accept 3D points with (x, y, z) coordinates. If you leave out the z-value of a point, as when using a pointing device such as a mouse, then AutoCAD uses the current *construction plane* or *elevation*.

Absolute coordinates: The system of absolute or Cartesian coordinates measures the position of any point as distances from the *origin* point (0, 0) which is initially at the lower left corner of the drawing. The use of negative coordinate numbers allows you to go to the left or to the bottom of the origin.

The coordinates of a point are always written or entered as x, y where the x distance (horizontal) is always given first followed by a comma. For example the coordinates (3, 4) specify a point which is located at 3 units to the right along the horizontal X-axis and 4 units up the vertical Y-axis. Decimal points can be used for accuracy.

When 3D points need to be specified, you use an additional Z-axis which is at right angles to the XY plane and has positive values coming 'out' of the screen. Coordinates are then expressed in the form *x, y, z*.

Relative coordinates: A point can also be specified as a set of distances along the axes from the *last point* rather than from the origin point. The 'at' sign @ must be used to signal that the following coordinates are relative.

For example, if the last point was (3, 4) then the entry @*2, 3.5* gives a new point of (5, 7.5). This method is useful for accurately entering the lengths of an object, such as a building. Movements in 3-dimensional space can also be given by relative coordinates.

Polar coordinates: An alternative form of relative coordinates specifies a point as the direct distance and angle compared to the last coordinates. The @ and the < signs must be used when entering the numbers. The 360 degrees of the circle are measured anticlockwise from the horizontal.

For example, the entry @*5<30* gives a new point that is 5 units from the last point, travelling in a direction at 30 degrees above the horizontal.

World coordinates: If you enter an asterisk (*) in front of the first part of any coordinate then the World Coordinate System will be used, overriding any different setting of the User Coordinate System.

UCS: The UCS command sets or changes the current User Coordinate System.

LOCATIONS

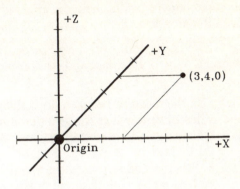

Absolute coordinates, Point 3,4,0

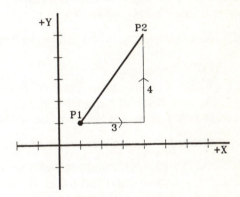

Relative coordinates @3,4

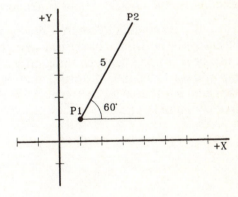

Polar coordinates @5<60

DRAWING AIDS

AutoCAD offers several tools which help the drawing process but which are not seen on the final paper copy. Most of these drawing aids can be quickly turned on, or off, by means of a function key.

GRID: The GRID command gives a grid of dots on screen with a spacing of your choice. The grid is only for reference and is not printed on paper. The Grid has various options:

Spacing(X)	Sets the distance between dots. Enter a number in drawing units. A value of zero makes the grid the same as the SNAP.
ON	ON. Turns grid on, using previous spacing.
OFF	OFF. Turns grid off.
Snap	S. Sets the grid setting to the SNAP setting.
Aspect	A. Sets a grid with different horizontal and vertical spacing.

SNAP: The SNAP command controls an invisible grid onto which all new points are locked. It is usually convenient to have the snap resolution set to the same value or to a similar value as the visible grid setting:

Spacing (X)	Sets the spacing of the snap grid. Enter a number.
ON	ON. Turns snap on.
OFF	OFF. Turns snap off.
Rotate	R. Rotates snap grid. Enter angle and give base point.
Aspect	A. Sets different horizontal and vertical spacings.
Style	S. Gives choice of Standard or Isometric grid.

The *Isometric* drawing grid uses axes set at 30, 90 and 150 degrees.

ISOPLANE: The ISOPLANE command also selects the isometric mode and offers cursor movement over the planes formed on the left, top or the right faces of a cube. Ctrl-E can often be used to set this mode.

AXIS: The AXIS command gives a display of ruler lines along the edges of the screen. Like the grid, these axes are for reference and are not produced on paper. The AXIS options are similar to the GRID options listed above.

ORTHO: The ORTHO command controls orthogonal drawing. While ortho mode is ON lines will always be horizontal or vertical, never diagonal. This can be a useful effect but it may also be confusing while pointing on screen and moving objects.

If the Snap grid is rotated then the ortho mode is also rotated. The ortho effect will also align itself with any special 'isometric plane' selected by the ISOPLANE command or by a SNAP command option.

DRAWING AIDS

Layer 0 Ortho Snap   3.000,5.000

Crosshairs

Grid points

Y-axis

User
Coordinates
Icon

X-axis

Snap

| X Spacing | 1.000 |
| Y Spacing | 1.000 |

Snap angle	0
X Base	0.000
Y Base	0.000

Snap	✓
Grid	✓
Axis	✓
Ortho	✓
Blips	✓

Isoplane

✓	Left
	Top
	Right

Grid

| X Spacing | 1.000 |
| Y Spacing | 1.000 |

Isometric

Axis

| X Spacing | 1.000 |
| Y Spacing | 1.000 |

OK   Cancel

Typical drawing screen and associated menu.

LAYERS

Different objects and parts of a drawing can be placed on different *layers* and controlled as a group. All dimensions, for example, can be kept on a single layer, given a special colour, and switched off when not wanted.

Layers are like a set of transparent overlays which are perfectly registered with one another. A drawing can have any number of layers, each with a particular name, colour and other properties. Information about layers is saved as part of the drawing.

There is always a 'current' layer on which newly drawn objects are placed. Until you choose otherwise, AutoCAD does all your drawing on a layer named '0' with a colour number of 7 (white) and a 'continuous' linetype.

Layers can be given names of your choice, up to 31 characters long. It is useful to have an organised system of layer names such as 'floor-1-windows', 'floor-1-electrical', etc.

LAYER: The LAYER command is used to create layers, to activate them, to change their properties and control their visibility.

?	Lists layers with their names and various properties.
Set	S. Selects a new current layer that already exists.
Make	M. Selects a new current layer, creating it if necessary.
New	N. Creates a new layer without affecting current layer.
OFF/ON	Selects layers to be turned off, or on again. Entities already drawn on an 'off' layer are not displayed or plotted.
Freeze/Thaw	Selects layers to be ignored during regeneration of drawings, allowing faster zoom and pan operations. Entities drawn on a 'frozen' layer are not displayed or plotted and can only be restored with the Thaw option.
Colour	C. Changes the colour number associated with selected layers.
Linetype	L. Changes the type of line associates with selected layers

Individual objects or entities can be given colours or linetypes which override the properties of the current layer. It is usually confusing to mix the two methods of control.

Every layer, or object, in a drawing is given a *colour number* between 1 and 255, or one of seven *colour names* (see illustration on Entities Prompt page). Although monochrome monitors cannot display the colours, the colour numbers and names are still required to drive different colour pens.

Related commands
CHANGE   Changes properties of selected objects.
COLOUR   Controls the colour of subsequent objects.
LINETYPE Controls the nature of the lines for subsequent objects.

LAYERS

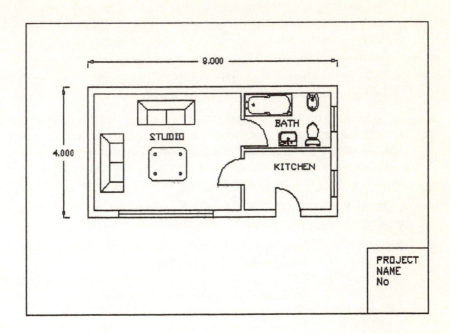

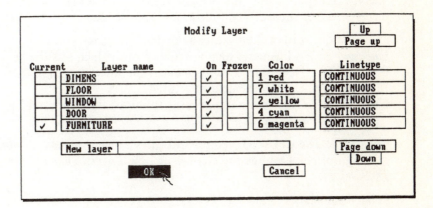

Layers. Typical drawing and menu showing layers.

ENTITIES

A complete drawing is built up from various smaller parts. A CAD *entity* is an object which you can create with a single command and which behaves as a single object on screen.

AutoCAD's entities include:

● Lines, Arcs, Circles, Points, Polylines, Traces, Solids, Traces, Shapes, Blocks, Text, Dimensions, Attributes, 3D Faces, 3D Meshes.

In addition to the shape that they make on screen, entities have various properties such as their Layer, Colour and Linetype, Elevation and Thickness. In AutoCAD words, 'thickness' is a 3-D term and not the 'width' of a line.

Entities can be given colours and linetypes either individually or by layer. To avoid confusion, it is usually best not to mix the two methods.

COLOUR/COLOR: The COLOUR command is used to set the colour of subsequently-drawn entities by using one of the the following options:

BYLAYER   New objects are drawn in the colour assigned to the current layer. Usually the default setting.
colour number Uses a number between 1 and 255 which produces standard colours for a particular type of display system.
colour name   Uses a standard name such as 'white' or 'red'.
BYBLOCK   Draws objects in white until they are grouped and inserted as a BLOCK.

LINETYPE: The LINETYPE command is used to set the continuous or dot-dash nature of subsequently-drawn lines, arcs, circles and polylines. Information about linetypes is kept in library files which can be created and loaded; otherwise the standard file of linetypes is used. The following responses can be given to the *set* option:

?   Lists the currently available linetypes.
Linename   A linename such as 'continuous' which sets the linetype.
BYLAYER   New objects are drawn in the linetype assigned to the current layer. Usually the default setting.
BYBLOCK   Objects are drawn in continuous linetype until they are grouped and inserted as a BLOCK.

CHANGE: The CHANGE command can change the position and the properties of existing objects. Options for change include *Layer*, *Colour*, *Linetype*, *Elevation* and *Thickness*.

Related commands
PEDIT   changes the characteristics of polyline entities.
LAYER   creates and controls the drawing layers.
LTSCALE   changes the length of the dashes in appropriate linetypes.

ENTITIES

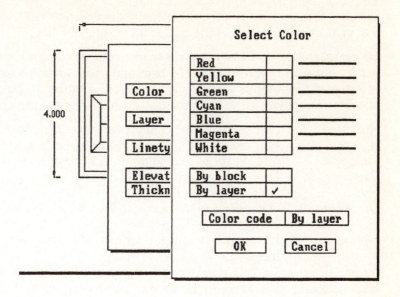

Typical entity properties.

ATTACHMENT

The computing power of AutoCAD can join lines and other entities with far greater accuracy than the hand and eye. The 'object snap' feature locks onto selected reference points of a drawing, such as the end or the middle of a line.

Object snap: An object snap option is requested by one of the methods given below. A 'target' box then appears on the crosshairs and when this box is used to pick on screen, object snap operation occurs on any object found within the box. If there are several possible snap points within the box then the one closest to the crosshairs is chosen.

Nearest	Nea. Snaps to the closest point on a line, arc or circle.
Endpoint	End. Snaps to the closest end of a line or arc.
Midpoint	Mid. Snaps to the midpoint of a line or arc.
Centre	Cen. Snaps to the centre of a circle or arc.
Node	Nod. Snaps to a Point.
Quadrant	Qua. Snaps to the closest 0, 90, 180, or 270 degree point of an arc or circle.
Intersection	Int. Snaps to the intersection of lines, arcs, circles or combinations of them.
Insert	Ins. Snaps to the insertion point of a Block, Text or Shape entity.
Perpendicular	Per. Snaps to the point on a line, arc or circle that makes a right angle with the last point.
Tangent	Tan. Snaps to the point on a circle or an arc that, connected to the last point, forms a tangent.
Quick	Qui. Snaps to the first object within the target box.
None	Turns off object snap.

Object snap can only operate on objects visible on screen. Regular Snap mode takes effect before object snap. Object snap overrides Ortho mode.

Override mode: This method takes effect for the current selection of a single point. It is activated within a command by picking the asterisk **** at the top of a menu or the Tools pull-down menu. The object snap does not effect the operation of the command.

Running mode: This method applies the object snap operation every time that a point is selected. The target box automatically appears at the centre of the crosshairs. Use the OSNAP command to turn this mode on, or off.

OSNAP: The OSNAP command is used to set running modes. Do not enter OSNAP before using override mode.

Related commands
APERTURE   controls the size of the target box for object snap operations.

ATTACHMENT

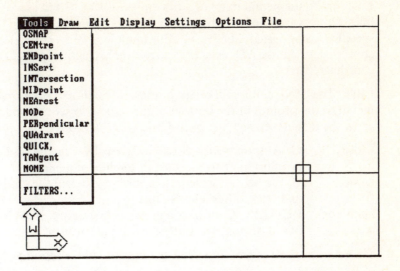

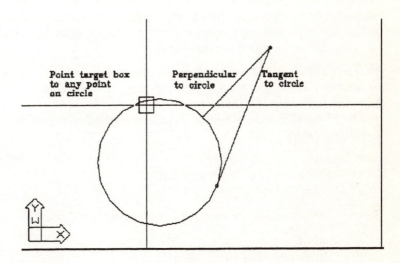

Object snap feature in use.

LINES AND POINTS

Lines are fundamental parts of a drawing and AutoCAD lets you build collections of lines, along with points or other types of mark. The positions of line and points can be specified using either 2D (x, y) coordinates or 3D (x, y, z) coordinates. For 2D coordinates, AutoCAD uses the current construction plane ('elevation') as the z-coordinate.

LINE: The LINE command offers you several methods of constructing a line. Read the menu, or the prompt at the bottom of the screen, to see the options. The <brackets> show the default setting; just press [RETURN] to accept it.

Close   C. Automatically closes a figure by drawing a line from the current position back to the start of the line sequence.
Undo   U. Erases the last length of the line. Repeat the Undo option to step back and erase other lengths, one by one.
Continue   RETURN. Continues a previous line or arc. Press RETURN or the space bar in response to the 'From point:' prompt.

The usual method of forming a line is to specify two endpoints, by pointing on screen or by entering coordinates. As you move the cross-hairs over the screen a dotted line stretches or 'rubber bands' from the first point. This effect stops when the end point of the line is chosen.

The LINE command remains 'active', ready for you to draw a connected line which will start on the last point of the first line. Otherwise press [RETURN], or the space bar, to end the line command. There is no difference between a set of connected lines created within a single LINE command and a similar set created by multiple use of the LINE command. Each line is a separate entity.

POINT: The POINT command places points in a drawing which can act as *nodes* for attachment with object snap. The points can also be given different types of display and size with following variables.

The PDMODE variable controls different visual effects at the point by entering the following values:

0	a dot	3	an X
1	nothing	4	a vertical line
2	a cross		

Adding further values draws extra figures around the point:

| 32 | a circle | 64 | a square |
| 96 | a circle plus a square. | | |

The PDSIZE variable controls the size of the point figure.

Related commands
PLINE   creates connected lines and arcs which behave as a single entity.
ARC   forms a curve by using part of a circle.

LINES AND POINTS

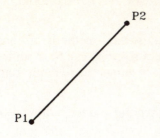

LINE — start and endpoints

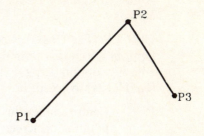

LINE — Continue option

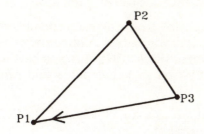

LINE — Close option

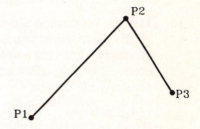

LINE — Undo option

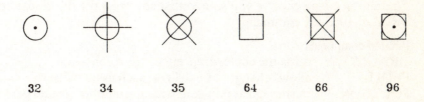

| 32 | 34 | 35 | 64 | 66 | 96 |

POINT — some PMODE settings

CIRCLES

AutoCAD makes it easy to construct circles and the flat-looking circles known as ellipses.

CIRCLE: The CIRCLE command offers several methods of constructing a circle. Options are chosen from the initial menu or a setting can be modified after starting by entering option letters. The <brackets> show the default setting – just press [RETURN] to accept it.

R   Centre and Radius. Uses the centre point and the radius given as a length or by pointing on screen.
D   Centre and Diameter. Uses the centre point and then the diameter entered as a length or by pointing on screen.
2P   2 Point. Uses the two end points of the diameter.
3P   3 Point. Uses any three points on the circumference of the circle.
TTR   Tangent, Tangent, Radius. Uses two lines or other objects which the circle will just touch, then the radius. Such a circle may not always exist.

The simplest method of drawing a circle is to give the centre point and the radius. If you specify the radius by pointing on screen you will see a dotted circle being 'dragged' over the display. Press the pointer button or [RETURN] when you have formed the desired circle. This drag effect may be slow on some computers and can be turned off if necessary.

ELLIPSE: AutoCAD builds an ellipse as a closed polyline. The ELLIPSE command allows you specify an ellipse by several options:

Axis   Default. Uses two ends of one axis and the length of other axis.
Centre   C. Uses the centre point, an endpoint of one axis and the length of other axis.
Rotation   R. Uses the rotation of a circle about first axis.
Isocircle I. Forms a circle in current isometric drawing plane, as set by the ISOPLANE command.

To draw an *elliptical curve* you should first construct the full ellipse and then use the TRIM or BREAK commands.

Related commands
DRAGMODE   turns the circle 'drag' effect off, or on again.
PEDIT   allows changes to polylines, such as an ellipse.
POLYGON   forms regular polygons with any number of sides between 3 and 1024.
ARC   forms a curve from part of a circle.
DONUT   or DOUGHNUT forms a filled circle or ring.

CIRCLES

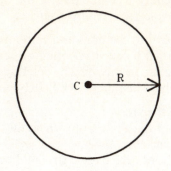

CIRCLE – centre and Radius

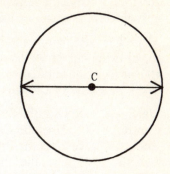

CIRCLE – centre and Diameter

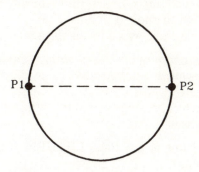

CIRCLE – 2 point

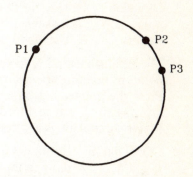

CIRCLE – 3 point

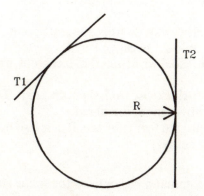

CIRCLE – Tangent, Tangent, Radius

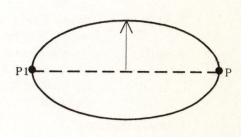

ELLIPSE – ends and length of axe

CURVES

An arc is a curve made from part of a circle. The tightness of the curve can be varied and different arcs can be joined together to form complex curves.

ARC: The ARC command offers you various methods and combinations of methods for drawing curves which are best learned by experimenting on screen. Options are chosen from the initial menu or a setting can be modified by entering the option letters. The <brackets> show the default setting – just press [RETURN] to accept it.

Start.	S. Uses the Start point of the arc.
Centre	C. Uses the Centre point of the circle from which the arc is made.
End	E. Uses the End point of the arc.
Length	L. Uses the length of the chord, which is the straight line between the start and end of the arc.
Angle	A. Uses the Angle included between the start and end of arc. Enter degrees, such as 90.
Direction	D. Uses the Direction which starts the arc. Enter the direction in degrees, such as 90, or by pointing to another point.
Radius	R. Uses the Radius of the circle which forms the arc.

The default method is to specify the curve by a *three-point arc* option. If you select points by pointing on screen then you will see a dotted curve being 'dragged' into shape. Press the pointer button, or [RETURN], to fix the shape. Alternative methods of drawing an arc can be directly started by choosing options from the initial ARC menu. Major combinations are described below.

CONTINUE	Continues a previous line or arc. Press RETURN or the space bar in reply to the first prompt.
S, C, E	The arc is formed around the centre point.
S, C, A	The arc is formed anti-clockwise from the start point, unless a negative angle is entered.
S, C, L	The arc is formed anti-clockwise from the start point. The minor arc (smallest) is formed unless a negative length is entered.
S, E, A	The arc is formed anti-clockwise from the start point, unless a negative angle is entered.
S, E, R	The arc is formed anti-clockwise from the start point. The minor arc is formed unless a negative length is entered.
S, E, D	The method can be used to form any arc. It can also be used to create a tangent to another entity.

Related commands

PEDIT	The polyline edit command has options for spline curves.
PLINE	creates connected lines and arcs which behave as a single entity.
DRAGMODE	turns the 'drag' effect off if it slows your computer.
ELLIPSE	can be used to form elliptical curves.
SKETCH	allows free-hand drawings.

CURVES

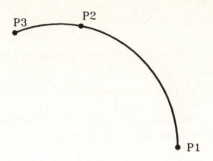

ARC − 3-Point

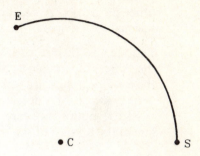

ARC − Start, Centre, End

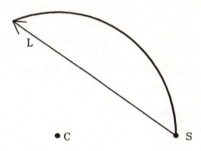

ARC − Start, Centre, Length

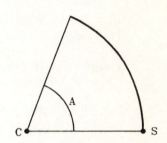

ARC − Start, Centre, Angle

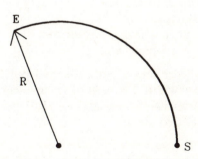

ARC − Start, End, Radius

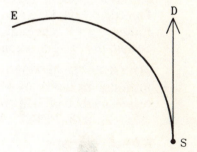

ARC − Start, End, Direction

POLYLINES

A polyline is a series of connected lines and curves which can have widths, tapers and other properties. A polyline object is a single entity so if any part of the polyline is selected for an operation, such as erasing, the complete entity will be affected.

PLINE: The PLINE command draws 2D polylines. It first asks for a start point and then offers the chance to enter the width of the line. This width is used for all parts of the polyline until you specify a different setting using one of the options. Joins between wide segments of a polyline are usually bevelled.

   PLINE options are chosen from the menu or by entering option letters at the prompt line at the bottom of the screen. The <brackets> on screen show the default setting.

Arc	A. Switches to the arc mode, described below.
Close	C. Automatically draws a line directly back to the start point and finishes the polyline. Use this option rather than drawing a closing line.
Length	L. Continues the next segment at the same angle to the previous segment, or as a tangent to an arc.
Width	W. The width of the next segment of polyline. Enter start width. End width is optional.
Halfwidth	H. The width from the centre of a wide polyline. Enter width as a value or by pointing.
Undo	U. Erases the last segment of the polyline. Repeating the option erases other segments, one by one.

Selecting the *Arc* option modifies some choices and offers extra options which are similar to those in the ARC command.

Line	L. Switches back to the line mode, described above.
Angle	A. The angle included between the start and end of arc. Enter degrees, such as 90. Negative values give a clockwise arc.
CEntre	CE. Overrides the normal centring action. Specify new centre.
CLose	CL. Closes the polyline with an arc.
Direction	D. Direction which starts the arc.
Radius	R. The radius of the circle which forms the arc.
Second pt	S. The second point of a 3-point arc.

3DPOLY: The 3DPOLY command creates a 3-dimensional polyline entirely made from straight line segments with zero width. The ends of the line segments are specified by any method of 3D point selection. The C(lose) and U(ndo) options have the same effects as in the PLINE command listed above.

Related commands
FILL	sets opaque filling of wide polylines to on or off.
PEDIT	allows changes to polylines: widths, breaks, joins, fit curves, spline curves.
LINE	creates simple lines.
ARC	creates simple curves.

POLYLINES

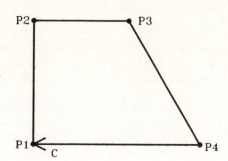

PLINE – Close option

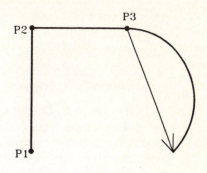

PLINE – Arc option

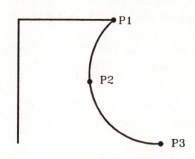

PLINE – 3-point Arc option

PLINE – repeated Arc option

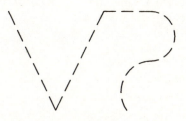

PLINE – dashed LINETYPE

PLINE – changes in Width option

2D SOLIDS

There are a number of drawing commands which give you control over the width of objects and whether or not the interior is filled in.

FILL: The FILL command controls the on/off mode of interior filling for Traces, Solids, and wide Polylines. Filling slows the action of some display screens and plotters. You can change the Fill mode at any time but existing objects will not change until the drawing is next regenerated. The current setting is remembered in the drawing file.

SOLID: The SOLID command lets you create 3-sided or 4-sided areas which can be filled. First and second points are used to draw a starting edge and the following two points form the next edge of a four-sided figure. The third point must be diagonally opposite the second point for a quadrilateral, otherwise a bow-tie shape is formed.

A triangular area is formed by pressing [RETURN] after specifying the third point. The command line waits for you to add another solid onto the first one. Press [RETURN] to finish the command.

TRACE: The TRACE command draws lines with a width which is specified when you start the command. You can set the width by entering a distance or by picking two points on screen. Traces are drawn solid unless the FILL command is set off.

The end points are on the centre line of a trace. The start and end of a trace are drawn square while the joins between segments are bevelled. The polylines created by the PLINE command produce the same effects as TRACE and are usually more versatile.

DOUGHNUT/DONUT: The DOUGHNUT or DONUT command is used to draw filled circles or rings. The prompt asks you to specify the diameter of the inside ring and the diameter of the outside ring.

The centre point of the doughnut can be 'dragged' and positioned on the screen. Press the pointer button when positioned. Press [RETURN] to end the command.

To produce a filled circle, enter 0 as the inside diameter.

Related commands

REGEN	fills solids, traces and polylines which were created with fill mode OFF.
PEDIT	allows changes to objects formed by the DOUGHNUT command.
DRAGMODE	turns the 'drag' effect off, or on again.

2D SOLIDS

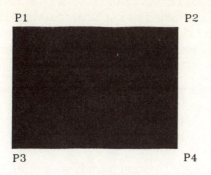

SOLID − 4−sided area

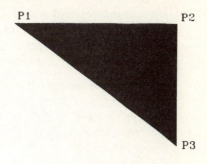

SOLID − 3−sided area

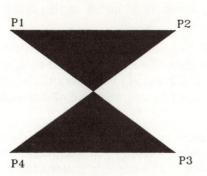

SOLID − 4−sided area

TRACE − with SOLID on

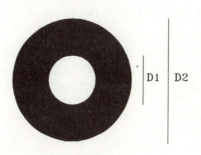

DOUGHNUT − open ring

DOUGHNUT − closed circle

3D SOLIDS

3DFACE: The 3DFACE command creates surfaces whose corners can have different z-coordinates and allows the construction of coplanar surfaces. The points of a 3D Face are specified in order, either clockwise or anti-clockwise.

The *Invisible* (I) option of a 3D Face allows you to make any edge or edges invisible. Enter the option just before the first point of that edge.

3D Polygon meshes: Polygon meshes are used to define flat surfaces or to construct approximate curved ones. The accuracy depends on the resolution of the mesh. A polygon mesh is defined by a matrix of *M* and *N* vertices although most of the commands described below automatically generate these vertices from selected lines and other objects.

The SURFTAB1 and SURFTAB2 system variables control the density of the generated mesh in the *M* and *N* directions.

3DMESH: The 3DMESH command constructs a 3D polygon mesh from a grid. You are prompted to specify the grid size of the M and N meshes and the location of each vertex using 2D or 3D coordinates.

RULESURF: The RULESURF command creates a polygon mesh constructed by ruled surface lines between two edges. You are prompted to select the edge entities which may be Lines, Points, Arcs, Circles, 2D Polylines or 3D Polylines.

The surface is constructed starting from the endpoint of each curve which is nearest to the pick point on the curve.

TABSURF: The TABSURF command creates a polygon mesh defined by a *path curve* line which is extruded along a *direction vector*. The path curve may be a Line, Arc, Circle, 2D Polyline or 3D Polyline. The surface is constructed starting at the point closest to the pick point.

REVSURF: The REVSURF command creates a surface of revolution by rotating a *path curve* around a defined *axis of rotation*. The path curve defines the *N* direction and may be a Line, Arc, Circle, 2D Polyline or 3D Polyline.

The degree to which the surface wraps around the axis is controlled by the start and the included angles.

EDGESURF: The EDGESURF command constructs a mesh surface between four adjoining edges. The shape of this *Coons surface patch* can be controlled by the nature of the Lines, Arcs or open Polylines which form the edge. These much touch at their *endpoints*.

The PEDIT command is used to change the properties of polygon meshes.

3D SOLIDS

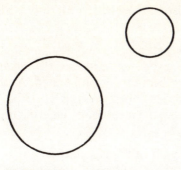

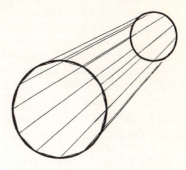

RULESURF – defining curves

RULESURF – ruled surface

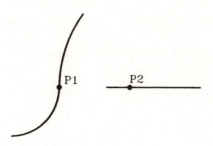

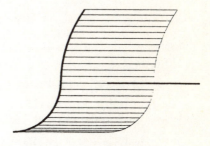

TABSURF – path curve and
direction vector

TABSURF – tabulated surface

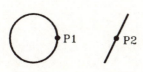

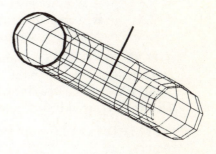

REVSURF – path curve and
axis of revolution

REVSURF – surface of revolution

TEXT

You can place text anywhere in an AutoCAD drawing and also give it various styles of characters (fonts) and sizes. Text can also be stretched, compressed, rotated and moved about.

TEXT: The TEXT Command asks for a start point and assumes that text is normally pushed to the left (left-justified). The text *height* and *rotation angle* can be entered, otherwise the default values shown in <brackets> will be used. At the 'Text' prompt you should type your characters and spaces, then press [RETURN].

Other Text options can be chosen from the menu or by entering the option letters at the prompt line.

Start point   Default. Starts text at the left of the baseline.
Align   A. Uses two endpoints of the baseline and fits text exactly between them.
Centre   C. Uses specified point to centre text.
Fit   F. Expands or contracts character width to that text exactly fits specified height.
Middle   M. Uses specified middle point to centre text both horizontally and vertically.
Right   R. Justifies text to right against specified point.
Style   S. Allows new text style to be specified. ? gives list of style names.

When you repeat the TEXT command you can press [RETURN] instead of entering a start point. AutoCAD will then start the new text on a new line below the previous text, and in the same style.

Control codes: Special character effects, such as underlining, are controlled by including the following control codes within your text.

%%u   turns underline on and off (use as a pair).
%%o   turns overscore on and off (use as a pair).
%%d   gives ° symbol for degrees.
%%p   gives 'plus/minus' symbol for tolerance.
%%d   gives 'diameter' symbol for circle.
%%%   gives single % symbol for percent.

DTEXT: The DTEXT command allows you to see text on the screen while you enter it. Otherwise it works in the same way as the TEXT command described above.

DTEXT starts a new line when you press [RETURN]. To cancel the command press [RETURN] again before entering any text, or use Ctrl-C.

STYLE: The STYLE command is used to create new styles or to modify existing style names.

A text style depends on the look of the font (the typeface), together with the size and angle of the characters. AutoCAD has standard fonts with names such as 'txt' (the default) and 'romans'. See Part 3 of the book for details of fonts.

TEXT

AutoCAD

TEXT,DTEXT – start point

AutoCAD

TEXT,DTEXT – Right option

AutoCAD

TEXT,DTEXT – Align option

AutoCAD

TEXT,DTEXT – Fit option

AutoCAD

TEXT,DTEXT – Centre option

AutoCAD

TEXT,DTEXT – Middle option

DIMENSIONS

Dimensioning is the addition of written lengths, distances or angles to objects on a drawing. AutoCAD can automatically add these dimensions including *associative* dimensions that stretch or otherwise adapt to changes in objects.

DIM, DIM1: The dimensioning process has a special 'Dim' prompt from which you only use dimensioning commands and options. Use the EXIT command or Ctrl-C to leave the dimensioning mode.

- The DIM1 command allows one dimensioning command before returning to normal command mode.
- The DIM command remains in dimensioning mode, ready for another dimension.

The various dimension commands and options prompt you to pick appropriate locations for the *extension lines* and the *dimension* lines. The measured length is displayed on the prompt line and is used as the *dimension text* by pressing [RETURN]. Any text can be entered from the keyboard and a single blank followed by [RETURN] suppresses the dimension text.

Linear dimensioning

HORIZONTAL	gives a horizontal dimension line.
VERTICAL	gives a vertical dimension line.
ALIGNED	gives a dimension line parallel to the origins of the extension lines.
ROTATED	gives a dimension line at a specified angle.
BASELINE	continues an offset dimension line from the baseline (first extension line) of the previous dimension.
CONTINUE	continues a dimension line from the second extension line of the previous dimension.

Angular dimensioning

ANGULAR   gives a dimension arc to show the angle between two non-parallel lines.

Diameter dimensioning

DIAMETER   gives a dimension line across the diameter of a circle or an arc.

Radius dimensioning

RADIUS   gives a dimension line across the radius of a circle or arc, with an optional centre mark.

Associative dimensioning

UPDATE	updates dimension entities to current setting of the dimension variables.
HOMETEXT	restores text to its default location.
NEWTEXT	changes the text of existing dimensions.

Options: Other dimensioning controls include CENTRE for marking the centre of circles and LEADER for controlling the placing of text. Dimensioning style can also be controlled by a large set of *dimensioning variables*, listed in Part 3 of the book.

DIMENSIONS

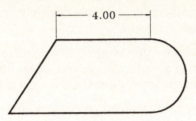

DIM – Linear dimension

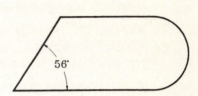

DIM – Angular dimension

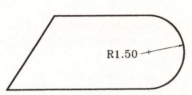

DIM – Radius dimension

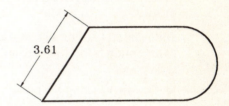

DIM – Aligned dimension

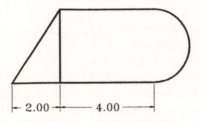

DIM – Continued dimension

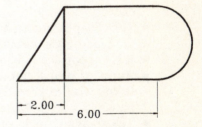

DIM – Baseline dimension

HATCHES AND PATTERNS

AutoCAD makes it easy for you to fill an area on a drawing with a crosshatched pattern. Hatches are usually ready-made patterns which conform with industry standards, but you can also create your own.

HATCH: The HATCH command has options which allow you to enter the *name* of a standard hatch pattern or to define a pattern while you work. Standard patterns are kept in a disk file which is part of the set of AutoCAD program files.

Name   Uses that name if it occurs in the *acad.pat* pattern library. Otherwise uses a matching *filename.pat*, if it exists.
?   Displays a list of the standard patterns in *acad.pat*.
U   Allows entry of a hatch definition by entry of the line angle, the line spacing, and crosshatching.

The boundaries for the hatched areas will be formed by the edges of objects which you select on screen. You can use any of the standard methods but selection by Window is often convenient. Press [RETURN] to complete the selection and start the hatching process.

Hatching styles: For all methods of pattern choice, the style of the pattern can be given as an option by adding a comma to the pattern name followed by one of the following style codes:

N   Normal (default). Hatching is switched off, and on again, at internal boundaries.
O   Outermost. Outer areas only are filled.
I   Ignore. Internal boundaries are ignored.

For example, the response *BRASS,I* hatches all areas within the boundary with the 'brass' pattern.

Hatch effects
- Empty spaces inside a boundary are completely filled with the chosen pattern.
- Objects which are inside the boundary, and which have *also* been selected, affect the hatching. The results depend on which of the hatching styles, listed above, has been chosen.
- Text, Shapes, Traces, Solids and Attributes are normally kept clear of hatching. Use the Ignore style to hatch through them.
- It is *not* possible to hatch inside an unfilled Trace or Solid.
- AutoCAD usually groups all the lines of one HATCH command into a single Block. If you wish to keep the lines as individual entities then use an asterisk after the pattern prompt – **BRASS*, for example.
- The standard angle of hatching can be set by the Rotate option of the SNAP command.
- Hatching around complex objects can be a slow process. Use Ctrl-C to interrupt the process if necessary.

HATCHES AND PATTERNS

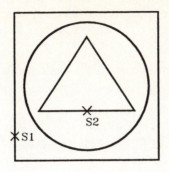

HATCH — selection of boundaries

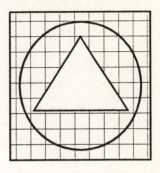

Effect of Normal style

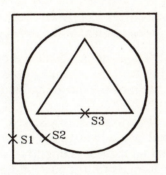

HATCH — selection of boundaries

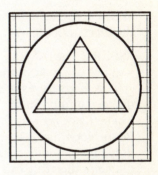

Effect of Normal style

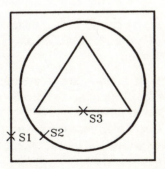

HATCH — selection of boundaries

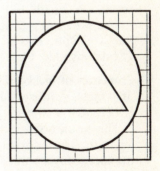

Effect of Outermost style

COMPONENT BLOCKS

A *Block* is a collection of objects on screen which have been grouped together and stored with a block name. You can group any set of objects as a block and use this 'part' many times again in the current drawing, or in other drawings. You can also import any block into a drawing from your 'library' of standard parts.

BLOCK: The BLOCK command creates new blocks while you work and stores them in the *current* drawing file.

- The *Block name* can be up to 31 characters long.
- The *Insertion base point* that you pick is used as the 'insertion point' or reference point for future insertions. The centre or the lower left corner of the Block is a useful base point.

The objects for the Block are selected by any of standard methods. When selection is complete the block is automatically saved and the objects in the block are removed from the screen. Use the OOPS command to recall the objects to the screen.

WBLOCK: The WBLOCK command behaves like the BLOCK command but stores the block as a separate drawing file, instead of within the drawing.

INSERT: The INSERT command inserts a previously-defined Block into your drawing and lets you control the position and scale of the incoming objects.

The *Insertion point* defines the position of the incoming block which can also be dragged into position.

The *Block name* is the name of the block as previously stored; use ? to obtain a list. If no block has been stored with that name then Insert looks outside the current drawing for another drawing file with that name and imports it as a Block. Complete drawings therefore can be brought in as parts for the current drawing.

The X and Y *scale factors* can be used to magnify or shrink all the X and Y dimensions of the incoming block. Negative numbers give mirror images. Press [RETURN] to accept the defaults of 1. Enter the *Rotation angle* or press [RETURN] to accept the default of no rotation.

The scale and rotation of a block can be pre-set before its insertion by entering the following options at the 'insertion point' prompt: Scale, Xscale, Yscale, Zscale, Rotate, PScale, PXscale, PYscale, PZscale, PRotate.

Properties of blocks: The components of a block are treated as a single entity in a drawing. Use an asterisk (*) in front of the block name to keep the entities separate. The EXPLODE command can also be used to separate entities.

The entities of a block can come from different layers with different colours and linetypes. This information is preserved within the block, except for entities drawn on the special layer named '0'.

Blocks may be 'nested' inside other blocks.

COMPONENT BLOCKS

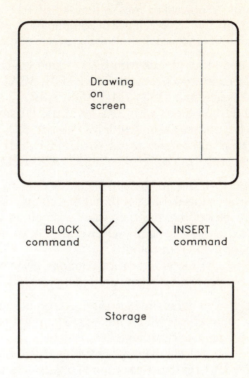

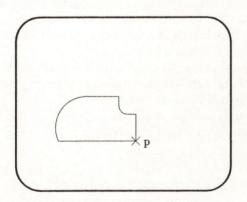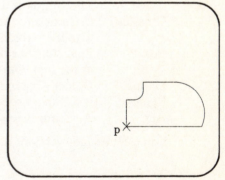

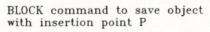

BLOCK command to save object
with insertion point P

INSERT command to import **object**
Xscale = −1 gives reversal

SELECT AND EDIT

Editing: All the objects or entities that AutoCAD draws on screen can be modified or 'edited'. You often have a choice of commands and techniques for an editing operation. The possibilities include the following effects and commands.

- Erase and recall objects with ERASE and UNDO.
- Change edges and sizes with STRETCH, SCALE, EXTEND and TRIM.
- Copy objects with COPY, MIRROR, ARRAY and OFFSET.
- Cut and trim objects with BREAK, DIVIDE and TRIM.
- Move the objects around with MOVE and ROTATE.
- Alter joins and corners with FILLET, CHAMFER and CHANGE.
- Change properties of polyline objects with PEDIT.

Object selection: Before you can change a drawing you need to 'select' the objects or entities to be changed. Most of the editing commands, such as erasing, ask you to *select objects* for processing and they share a common system of picking objects. Objects which have been successfully selected are shown on screen in special display such as with dots or a different colour.

The selection process has various options, given below, and a mixture of options can be used. No processing begins until you press [RETURN].

Pointing	This default method uses a target box at the centre of the cursor and selects an object within the box. The point can also be typed in as absolute or relative coordinates.
Last	L. Selects the most recently-created object visible on screen.
Previous	P. Uses the same group of objects selected during the last selection process.
Window	W. Selects all objects which are completely contained within the rectangular screen box made with two corner points.
Multiple	M. Sets the selection to scan the drawing just once for a group of objects. This option is useful to select two objects which intersect.
Crossing	C. Similar to the Window option but selects objects which are contained within *or* crossing the window boundary.
Box	Box. Acts like the Window option if second corner of box is to the right of the first. Otherwise acts like the Crossing option.
Undo	U. Steps back through selection process.
Remove	R. Changes selection to remove objects.
Add	A. Changes selection back to adding objects.

Some commands versions have fewer options.

SELECT AND EDIT

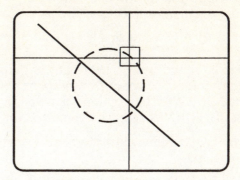

Selection by Pointing

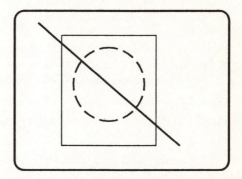

Selection by Window

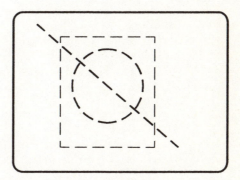

Selection by Crossing

ERASE AND UNDO

AutoCAD allows you to 'rub-out' unwanted parts of your drawing. You can also recover from commands which give unwanted or unexpected effects.

ERASE: The ERASE command gives control over the removal of parts of your drawing.

Objects to be erased are selected by any of the standard methods such as pointing with the target form of cursor or by windowing – see the Select and Edit prompt page for full details. The *L* for Last option is a useful way of erasing the entity you have just drawn. Use [RETURN] to repeat the command and repeat the effect of the Last option.

OOPS: The OOPS command restores all the objects removed in the most recent ERASE command.

UNDO: The UNDO command allows you to retrace a sequence of commands and undo their effects, one by one. The command has various options:

Number   x. Enters the number of commands to step back.
Auto   A. Groups any item into a single command which can be reversed by a single U.
Mark   M. Places a marker in the undo information for the Back option.
Back   B. Performs UNDO effects back to previous Mark.
Control   C. Disables or limits the UNDO command.

U: The U command undoes the most recent AutoCAD operation and is equivalent to the UNDO 1 command. The U command can be repeated and backs up one command at a time.

REDO: The REDO command undoes the effect of an UNDO or U command. It must be entered immediately after command.

REDRAW: The REDRAW command refreshes the screen display and removes marks left by erased objects.

ERASE AND UNDO

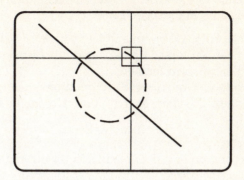

ERASE – selection of object

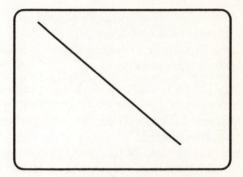

Effect of ERASE command

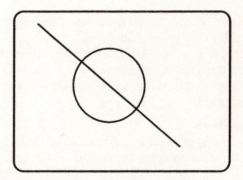

OOPS – restores last erasure

CUTS AND OPENINGS

AutoCAD allows you to use a variety of techniques for cutting, trimming, splitting and making openings in objects.

BREAK: The BREAK command lets you erase part of a Line, Arc, Circle, Trace or Polyline. It can also make a gap or split an object into two parts. You select the object by any of the standard methods.

When you select an object with a pointing device, such as a mouse, it is assumed that the break point also starts at that point. Use the **First** option to specify a different first point.

Break effects
- If the second point is not actually on the object then the nearest point on the object is used for the break.
- If the second point is beyond one end of a line or arc, then that end is cut off.
- A circle is changed to an arc. The deletion takes place in an anti-clockwise direction from the first to the second point.
- To split an object, without a gap, the second point must be the same as the first point. Enter @ to repeat the first coordinate.
- A polyline is broken in a similar manner to a line or arc. A polyline with width is given cuts with square ends.

TRIM: The TRIM command cuts objects in a drawing so that they end precisely at the edge of another object. Use any of the standard methods to select the *cutting edge*, or edges, then press [RETURN]. The selected edges are highlighted but these objects will not themselves be trimmed.

Then select the objects to be trimmed by pointing to the part which is to be trimmed. Select further objects if required, then press [RETURN] to complete the command.

Trim effects
- Trimming takes place at the intersections of the cutting edges and the selected objects.
- If a selection point is between the end of the object and an intersection then the object is cut back to the intersection.
- If a selection point is between two intersections then TRIM deletes the part of the object between the intersections.
- Polylines are trimmed on their centre lines. If the width is tapered then the trimmed end is adjusted.

Related commands
EXTEND   lengthens a Line, Arc or Polyline to meet another object
ERASE   deletes a complete entity.
DIVIDE   splits an entity into a specified number of parts of equal length.

CUTS AND OPENINGS

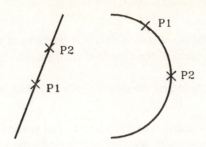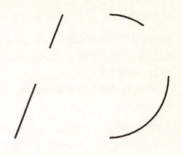

BREAK – selection of points   Effects of BREAK command

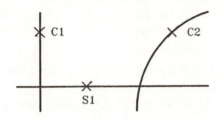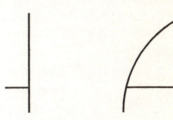

TRIM – cutting edges C1 & C2   Effect of TRIM command
and object to trim S1

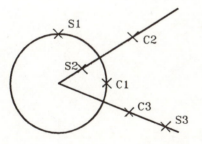

TRIM – multiple cutting edges, C   Effects of multiple TRIM command
and objects to trim, S

MOVES AND TURNS

Objects in your drawings can be completely moved to a new position or rotated about any point.

MOVE: The MOVE command moves objects to a new position in a drawing without changing their size or orientation. Use any of the standard methods to select the objects to be moved.

You specify the movement of the selected objects by two types of entry described below.

Two points   Enter a first base point and a second point. The points can be picked on screen and the movement seen by dragging to the second point.

Displacement   Press [RETURN] for the second point. The first entry is used as a relative set of x,y distances.

ROTATE: The ROTATE command changes the direction which any object faces. The object is selected by any of the standard methods and a base point is picked, about which the turning will take place. A point on a corner of the object is usually easiest to control but the base point doesn't have to be on the selected object.

You specify the amount of rotation or the turning effect by several methods given below. Angles are measured from an imaginary horizontal line passing through the base point.

Rotation angle   Default method. Enter degrees. Positive angles cause anti-clockwise rotation and negative angles cause clockwise rotation.

Reference   R. Uses the current rotation and the desired new rotation. Enter degrees.

The drag mode lets you see see the rotation taking place. Check that ORTHO has been set to OFF.

MOVES AND TURNS

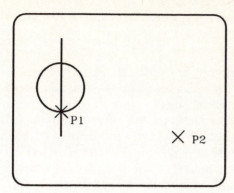

MOVE – by selection of points

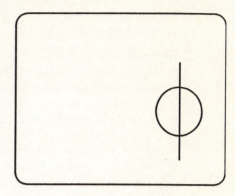

Effect of MOVE command

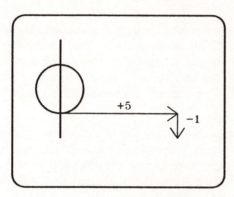

MOVE – by entry of displacements

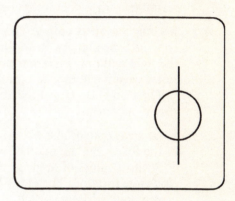

Effect of MOVE command

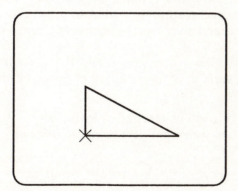

ROTATE – selection of base point

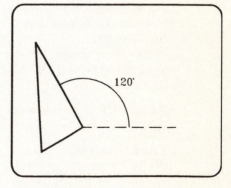

Effect of ROTATE command with angle of +120 degrees

COPIES

COPY: The COPY command makes duplicates of objects in a drawing and leaves the original objects intact. The copies are scaled and orientated like the originals and are independent of the originals.

Copy effects
- Objects for copying are selected by any of the standard methods. You then pick a base point as the first point from which the new position is measured. The base point does not have to be on the original object.
- The copy is dragged on the screen until the second point is picked. If a [RETURN] is made as the second entry then the first entry will be used as the displacement or relative x,y distances between the original and the copied object.
- The *Multiple option* (M) allows multiple copies of the original object by repeating the prompt for the second point. The base point is kept the same.

ARRAY: The ARRAY command makes multiple copies of selected objects in a rectangular or a polar (circular) pattern.

Rectangular array option: This option uses horizontal Rows and vertical Columns to construct the pattern. Rows and Columns are entered as whole numbers measured to the right and upwards from the first or 'cornerstone' element in the lower left corner. Enter negative numbers to build the array to the left or below the first element.

The Rotate option of the SNAP command can be used to rotate the base line of a rectangular array.

Polar array option: This option uses the centre point of the circular pattern and any two of the following: the number of items, the angle to fill, and the angle between items.

Positive values of angle give an anti-clockwise rotation and negative angles give a clockwise rotation. The individual objects in the final array can be rotated around the centre point (default) or left in their original orientation.

MIRROR: The MIRROR command makes inverted images of any selected objects in your drawing. The mirror effect takes place around a line which you specify by picking two points on screen. The command gives you the option of keeping or deleting the original object.

The mirror image follows the laws of reflection and the effect on Text can be controlled by the MIRRTEXT variable of the SETVAR command with the following effects:

MIRRTEXT=1 (the default). Text will be reversed or inverted.
MIRRTEXT=0. Text is kept true, with equivalent layout to original.

Related commands
OFFSET   creates an identical curve or line in a parallel position.

COPIES

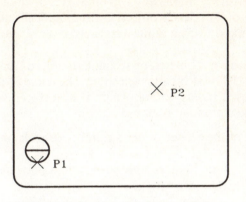

COPY – selection of base points

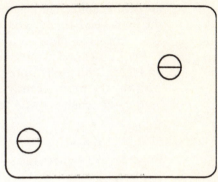

Effect of COPY command

ARRAY – Rectangular option

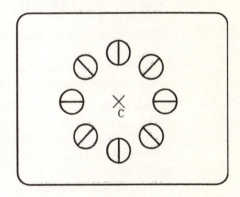

ARRAY – Polar option

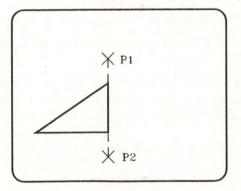

MIRROR – selection of mirror line

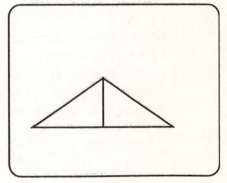

Effect of MIRROR command with original object kept

JOINS

FILLET: The FILLET command connects any two lines, arcs or circles with a curved arc of any radius. The lengths of the selected objects are automatically adjusted to make the join. The FILLET command, with a radius set to zero, is also useful for making sharp-cornered joins.

FILLET expects you to select *two* objects, or straight sections of the same polyline, and there is no need to press [RETURN] after selection. The curve of the join is made with the the most recently-used radius setting, which is also stored with a drawing. Settings are changed with the command options.

Radius   R. Sets the radius of the corner. Enter a number or pick two points on the screen.

Polyline   P. Applies the same fillet to all eligible corners in a polyline.

Fillet effects

- When two points are on the same polyline they must be adjacent or separated by one other segment. The FILLET operation replaces the intermediate segment with a fillet curve.
- Fillet curves can be made between two circles, two arcs, a line and circle, a line and arc.
- If there is more than one possible fillet between objects, FILLET chooses the one with endpoints closest to the two points used for selection.

CHAMFER: The CHAMFER command makes a flattened corner between two lines which intersect, or could intersect. The operation and the effects of the CHAMFER command are similar to those of the FILLET command.

The start and end points of the chamfer line are given by the distances measured from the intersection point of the two lines. These distances are remembered for future CHAMFER commands and are also stored in the drawing file.

Distances   D. Sets the slope of the chamfer line. Enter a distance from the intersection point, or pick points on screen.

Polyline   P. Applies the same chamfer to all eligible points on a polyline.

When a polyline is chamfered, the second line must be adjacent to the first, or separated by one other segment.

CHANGE: The CHANGE command lets you change various properties of selected entities such as Line, Circle, Text and Blocks. The default option is *change point* and its effect depends on the type of objects selected. For a line, the endpoint is moved to the change point.

Several lines can adjusted to join at the same change point.

JOINS

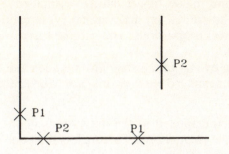 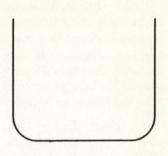

FILLET – selection of points   Effects of FILLET command

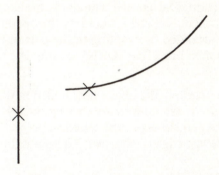 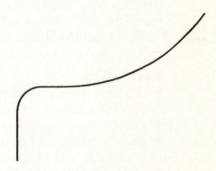

FILLET – selection of points   Effect of FILLET command

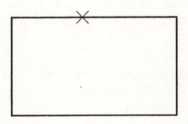 

CHAMFER – selection of polyline   Effect of CHAMFER command

EXPAND AND CONTRACT

SCALE: The SCALE command makes objects larger or smaller. The same scaling factor is applied to both the horizontal (x) and vertical (y) directions so the object expands or contracts with correct proportions. You can use this command to change the scale of entire drawings.

Select the objects for scaling by any of the standard methods and then pick a base point. The base point remains unchanged but does not have to be on the selected object. Use the following options:

Scale factor   Default. The factor applied to the dimensions of the object. Factors greater than 1 give enlargement. Factors less than one give reduction.

Reference   R. Uses a reference length which can be entered or picked on screen. Enter the desired new length or drag object on screen.

EXTEND: The EXTEND command lengthens objects in a drawing so that they end at the edge of another object. Select the *boundary edge*, or edges, first, then press [RETURN] to complete the selection. The selected boundary objects are highlighted on screen but these objects will not themselves be affected by the operation.

Then select the objects to be extended by pointing to the part of the object. Select further objects, if required, and then press [RETURN] to complete the command.

Extend effects
* If several boundary edges are selected, the object is extended to the first boundary. An object may be picked again to extend it to another boundary.
* Objects are extended from the end closest to the selection point.
* For a polyline, the first or the last edge is extended. The centre line of the polyline is extended to the boundary.
* Only open polylines can be extended.
* If a polyline is used as a boundary, objects are extended to its centre line.

STRETCH: The STRETCH command stretches or shrinks objects. It moves the position of selected *parts* of a drawing and preserves the connections with the parts left in place. You can select multiple objects but the Window or Crossing must be used at least once. The amount of stretch is chosen by picking any base point and a new point, which can be dragged on screen.

Stretch effects
* Objects entirely within the selection window are completely moved.
* For objects which cross the window, only those endpoints within the window are moved, leaving other endpoints unchanged.

EXPAND AND CONTRACT

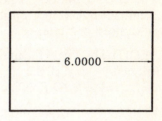

SCALE – selection of base point

Effect of SCALE command with scale factor of 2

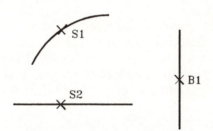

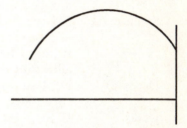

EXTEND – boundary edges B1 and selected objects S1 & S2

Effects of EXTEND command

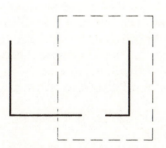

STRETCH – window selection of objects

Effect of STRETCH command

POLYLINE CHANGES

The Polyline entities of 2D Polylines, 3D Polyline and meshes have special editing commands. A 'vertex' is the point where two parts of a Polyline meet; the plural word is 'vertices' or 'vertexes'.

PEDIT: The PEDIT command operates on Polylines and meshes which have been selected by any of the standard methods. Entities which are not a polyline can be converted to a 2D Polyline by this method.

Close	C. Connects the last segment with the first to make a closed figure.
Open	O. Removes the last segment of a closed Polyline.
Join	J. Adds to a current open Polyline any other Lines, Arcs and Polylines which meet the Polyline at either end.
Width	W. Sets a new uniform width for the entire Polyline. Enter a figure or specify two points on screen.
Edit vertex	E. Switches to the Vertex editing, described below.
Fit curve	C. Forms a smooth curve to fit all points on the Polyline. Uses pairs of arcs between vertices.
Spline curve	S. Forms a *B-spline* curve using the vertices of the Polyline as a frame of control points. The curve passes through the start and end point and is 'pulled' towards the other points. The SPLINETYPE system variable allows quadratic and cubic B-splines to be generated.
Decurve	D. Restores a Polyline to the form it had before Fit curve or Spline curve operations.
Undo	U. Steps back and reverses PEDIT operations.
Exit	X. Returns to the main Command: prompt.

Vertex editing: The *(E)dit vertex* option of the PEDIT marks the position of the current vertex with an 'X' on the screen. An arrow also shows the tangent direction, if you specified one. The following options are then available.

Next, Previous	N,P. Steps the 'X' marker to the next or previous vertex
Break	B. Splits the Polyline into two pieces at a specified point or points. Any segments and vertices between the points are deleted. Use (N)ext to specify a second point; use the (G)o sub-option to specify a break point; use e(X)it to cancel Break operation.
Insert	I. Adds a new vertex to the Polyline at specified position after the current vertex.
Move	M. Moves the marked vertex to another location.
Regen	R. Regenerates the Polyline.
Straighten	S. Changes specified segments with one straight segment. Enter vertices.
Tangent	T. Attaches a tangent direction to the current vertex.
Width	W. Changes the start and end widths for the segment following the current vertex.
eXit	X. Returns to the main Command: prompt.

3D Polylines: If a 3D polyline is selected the PEDIT command offers options with similar effects to the 2D options. The Spline curve option fits a a 3D B-spline to the control points.

POLYLINE CHANGES

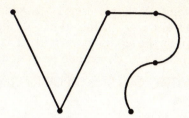

Original Polyline

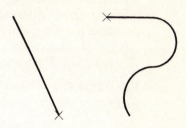

PEDIT – Break option

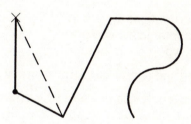

PEDIT – Insert option

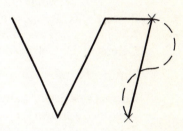

PEDIT – Straighten option

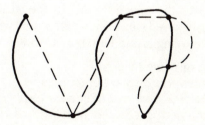

PEDIT – Fit curve option

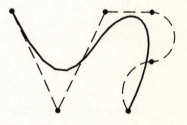

PEDIT – Spline curve option

SPLIT SCREENS

AutoCAD allows you to split the graphics screen into *viewport* areas which display different views of the same drawing. A simple use of this feature is to display the complete drawing while you also work on a magnified part of the drawing. Different types of 3D view can also be shown on the separate viewports. The number of available viewports usually ranges between 4 and 16, depending on your system.

VIEWPORTS, VPORTS: The VIEWPORTS or VPORTS command controls the number of viewports on the screen.

n	2, 3, 4. Divides the current viewport into 2, 3 or 4 viewports. Vertical and horizontal options available.
Single	SI. Returns to a single viewport using the view of the current viewport.
Join	J. Combines two adjacent viewports into one using the view of the dominant viewport.
Save	S. Assigns a name to the current viewport configuration and saves it with the drawing.
Restore	R. Restores a saved viewport configuration.
?	Displays information about active viewports.
Delete	D. Deletes a named viewport configuration.

Different combinations of dividing and joining can form a variety of viewport layouts.

Current viewport: At any time there is only one viewport which is active and this current viewport is shown by a heavy border and the presence of the cursor. You can change the active viewport by moving the cursor and picking with the pointing device. In most cases you can change the viewpoint in mid-command.

Viewport lock: The following commands limit cursor movement to the current viewport while the command is in progress:

SNAP, GRID, ZOOM, PAN, VPOINT, DVIEW, VIEWPORTS.

VIEW: The VIEW command saves the screen display of the current viewport as a named view and retrieves previously-saved views. Views are stored with the drawing file and are a convenient method of moving around a large drawing.

?	gives a list and details of named views.
Save	S. Saves the current viewport display. Enter a name.
Window	W. Uses window corners to save part of current display without zooming.
Restore	R. Replaces the current viewport display with a stored view. Enter a name.
Delete	D. Removes a named view.

Related commands

REDRAW	forces a redraw of the current viewport.
REDRAWALL	forces a redraw of all multiple viewports.
REGEN	forces a regeneration of the current viewport.
REGENALL	forces a regeneration of the all multiple viewports.

SPLIT SCREENS

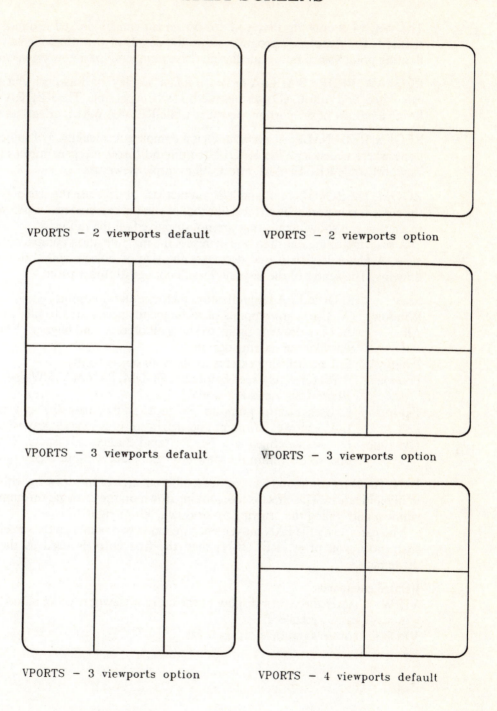

VPORTS – 2 viewports default   VPORTS – 2 viewports option

VPORTS – 3 viewports default   VPORTS – 3 viewports option

VPORTS – 3 viewports option   VPORTS – 4 viewports default

VIEW CHANGES

The view of a drawing that you see on screen can be moved around, enlarged or reduced. The AutoCAD program stores the details of your drawing as very accurate floating point values but recalculating these numbers, for a new view, can take time.

REDRAW, REDRAWALL: A *redraw* is a fast 're-play' of drawings which are already calculated, and AutoCAD uses this method where possible. The REDRAW command forces a redraw of the current viewport while REDRAWALL affects all viewports.

REGEN, REGENALL: A *regeneration* is a complete recalculation of values and is only done where necessary. The REGEN command forces a regeneration of the current viewport while REGENALL affects all multiple viewports.

ZOOM: The ZOOM command lets you increase or decrease the size of objects within the current viewport. The effect is like that of a zoom camera lens. When you 'zoom in' the screen can show details that are not displayed on the full view.

A scale factor greater than one increases the magnification compared to the *current* view. A factor less than one decreases the size of objects and shows more of the drawing. The centre of the display doesn't change during a zoom.

Scale	x. Default. A magnification factor. Enter a number.
Window	W. Uses corner points of rectangle to specify area to fill screen.
All	A. Uses drawing limits to show all objects, and beyond. For 3D views it acts like the Extents option.
Extents	E. Uses drawing extents to show all objects only.
Previous	P. Restores view seen before last ZOOM, PAN or VIEW operations. Up to 10 previous views are stored.
Centre	C. Uses a centre point and height to show a new display window.
Left	L. Uses lower left point and height to show new display window.
Dynamic	D. Uses a defined *view box* for rapid changes of display. ZOOM or PAN operations within the view box take place without regeneration.

PAN: The PAN command lets you see a different area of the drawing without a change in magnification. The effect is like looking down on the drawing through a stationary window and sliding the drawing up or down, left or right.

You can specify the PAN movement by picking two points on the screen. If, after the first entry, you press [RETURN] then the first entry is used as the relative x,y movement.

Related commands

VIEW	stores the screen display of the current viewport using named views which can be recalled.
VPORT	controls multiple screen areas.

VIEW CHANGES

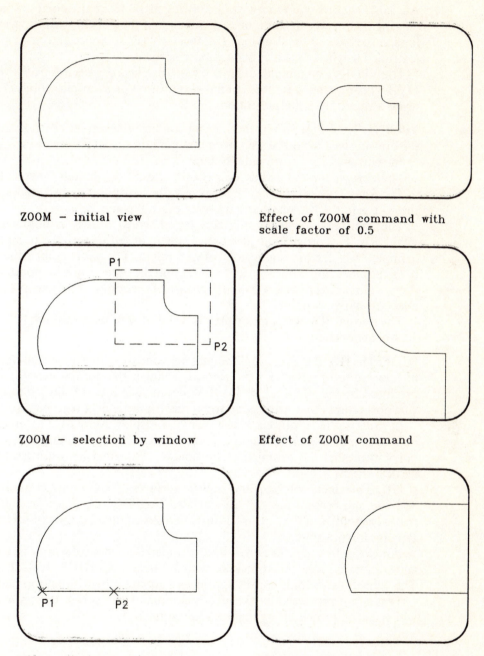

ZOOM – initial view

Effect of ZOOM command with scale factor of 0.5

ZOOM – selection by window

Effect of ZOOM command

PAN – displacement points

Effect of PAN command

3D VIEWS

AutoCAD allows you to view your drawing in 3D from any point in space. From the viewing point you can continue to create or edit the drawing and suppress the view of lines at the back of the drawing. You will only get 3D representations if the thickness (extruded height) of each entity has been specified.

The VPOINT command, described here, displays objects in *parallel projection*. The DVIEW command, described on the next prompt page, displays objects in *perspective* using a vanishing-point projection.

VPOINT: The VPOINT sets the viewing point for the current viewport and re-displays the drawing as it would be seen from that point in space. Points and angles are relative to the current User Coordinate System.

The *view point* is entered as *x,y,z* coordinates of the desired viewpoint.

The *Rotate* option allows you to specify the view point by two angles: around from the X-axis in the XY plane and up from the XY plane.

The alternative *compass* and *axes tripod* screen display is obtained by pressing RETURN. This provides an alternative system of setting the view point by means of a 'compass' which represents a globe of view points. The centre point is the north pole (0, 0, 1), the inner ring is the equator (n, n, 0), and the outer ring is the south pole (0, 0, –1). As you move the crosshairs over the surface of the compass the axes rotate to show the effect of that view point.

The normal 2D viewpoint or plan is restored with the viewpoint 0, 0, 1 or with the PLAN command.

HIDE: The HIDE command eliminates lines and other entities which would would not be seen from a particular view point. It changes the normal wire-frame 3D display produced by the VPOINT or DVIEW commands into a solid-looking display. The viewport returns to a wire-frame when the display is next regenerated.

In order to 'hide' objects at the rear of a display AutoCAD assumes that certain objects cannot be seen through. Circles, Solids, Traces, wide Polylines, 3D Faces and polygon meshes are assumed to be opaque. Extruded lines are treated as opaque vertical sheets.

HIDE produces solid top and bottom surfaces on some entities and not on others. The top and bottom faces of an extruded Circle, Solid, Trace or wide Polyline are treated as solid. But the top and bottom of a closed figure drawn with Lines or a closed Polyline are not solid.

For example, a cube drawn as four extruded lines looks the same in wire-frame as a cube drawn as an extruded Solid or with 3D Faces, but HIDE treats them differently. The cube drawn with lines will appear as a square tube without top and bottom.

Text is not processed by the HIDE command and is best put on a separate layer which can be turned off by the LAYER command.

3D VIEWS

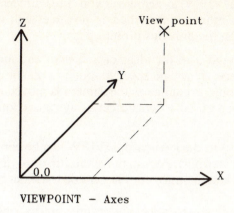

VIEWPOINT – Axes

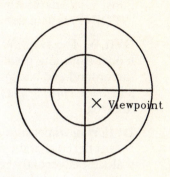

VIEWPOINT – Compass

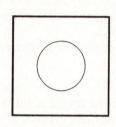

VIEWPOINT – Plan view

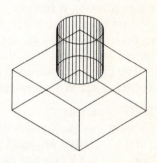

VIEWPOINT – view from 1,–1,1

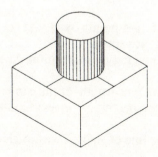

HIDE – effect upon base
created by LINE command

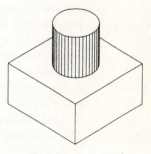

HIDE – effect upon base
created by SOLID command

PERSPECTIVE VIEWS

AutoCAD's Dynamic View (DVIEW) system gives you three-dimensional 'visualisations' of your drawing with more control than is possible with the View Point (VPOINT) system described on the previous prompt page.

DVIEW: The DVIEW command uses the ideas of a *camera* and *target* to view the model from any point in space. When perspective mode is on the relative sizes of foreground and background objects change as the camera is moved in or out. Front and back *clipping planes* can be used to create cut-away or section views of your drawing.

DVIEW operations: In addition to the keyboard, DVIEW can be controlled by *slider bars* at the edge of the current viewport. As you move the cursor to different angles or scales the effect of that change is seen on screen. The zero on the slider bar is the current viewpoint.

The DVIEW command allows you to 'select objects' in your drawing which are then stretched about on screen as you change views. On completion of the command the entire drawing is regenerated to give the new view.

If no objects are selected then AutoCAD temporarily displays a simple 'house' on screen to show you effects of different views. You can define you own standard test object and store it as a block called *DVIEWBLOCK*.

The DVIEW command uses points and angles relative to the current UCS unless the WORLDVIEW system variable is set to 1.

DVIEW options

Camera	CA. Rotates the viewing point about the target point. Use slider bars or enter angles. The first sequence of movement is up or down relative to the XY plane of the current UCS. The second movement is the rotation around the target, measured from the X axis.
Target	TA. Rotates the point being viewed about the line of sight. The sequence is similar to the Camera option.
Distance	D. Moves the camera in or out along the line of sight. This option turns *perspective viewing* on.
Points	PO. Locates the camera and target points by (x,y,z) coordinates. Parallel projection is used while points are specified.
Pan	PA. Moves the image with changing magnification. Specify distance and direction.
Zoom	Z. If perspective on, adjusts the 'lens length' of the camera. Longer lengths give a telephoto lens effect. If perspective off, gives a similar effect to regular ZOOM Centre command.
Twist	TW. Tilts the view around the line of sight. Twist angle is measured anti-clockwise.
Clip	CL. Specifies front and back *clipping planes* which act like invisible walls. The camera position is the default front plane. Default clipping option is O(ff).
Hide	Suppresses hidden lines on the objects selected for preview.
Off	Turns perspective off. See also Distance option.
Undo	U. Reverses effect of last DVIEW option.
Exit	X. Ends the DVIEW command and regenerates entire drawing.

PERSPECTIVE VIEWS

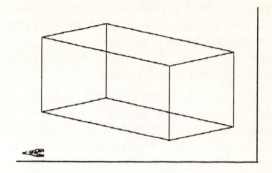

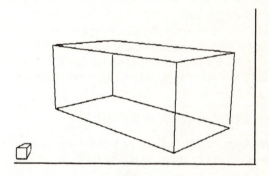

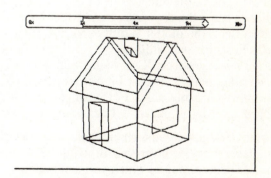

DVIEW command – effects before and after.

PLOTTING AND PRINTING

AutoCAD makes paper copies of your drawings on the make of plotter or printer that you chose when installing the program. *Plotters* use pens of different colours and are available for paper sizes from A4 to A0. Plotters are accurate but a large detailed drawing may take hours to produce.

Printer plotters are dot-matrix or laser printers which usually give a rapid monochrome printout on A4 paper.

PLOT, PRPLOT: The PLOT command starts the output routine for a pen plotter The PRPLOT command starts the output routine for a printer plotter.

Plotting may also be started from the Main Menu. The plotting routine offers options, described below which give you a chance to control the view, the scale and other parameters of your drawing. Your first plots or prints will usually be trials which you should use to change the parameters for future work. Use Ctrl-C to cancel the plot at any time. Settings will be remembered for the next plot.

Display   D. Plots the view seen on screen just before the last SAVE or END command.
Extents   E. Plots only the drawing area which contains entities.
Limits   L. Plots the entire drawing area defined by the drawing limits.
View   V. Plots a named view saved by the VIEW command.
Window   W. Plots area defined by corner points of a rectangle.

The following options can also be changed. Current settings are shown in brackets and can be accepted by pressing RETURN:

Plot files store the drawing and can be used by some software to plot the drawing at another some other time, or in the background.
Inches or millimetres are the units used for plot specifications.
Plot origin is normally the lower left corner of the paper but can be changed by entering the X,Y distance from the corner.
Plotting size affects the dimensions of the drawing on the paper.
Plot rotation turns the drawing on the paper by 90 degrees.
Pen width affects the plotter action needed to fill a solid area.
Area fill adjusts for pen width when plotting solid objects.
Hidden line removal affects 3D drawings and may cause a large increase in plotting time.
Plot scale either makes the best Fit onto the paper or lets you set the scale in the form: Plotted units=Drawing units. For example, if 1 drawing unit on screen represents 1 metre then 20 mm (on paper) = 1 drawing unit gives an architectural scale of 1:50.

Pens: AutoCAD gives you a chance to change details of the pens for some models of plotter. Each entity or layer in a drawing has a colour 'number' or 'name' (see the appropriate prompt pages) which you can match to the pens actually in your plotter.

Keep the the plotter linetype set at 'continuous, and use the CHANGE or LINETYPE commands to obtain dashed or dotted lines.

PLOTTING AND PRINTING

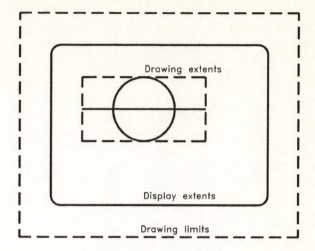

Printing boundaries.

```
Plot will NOT be written to a selected file
Sizes are in Millimeters
Plot origin is at (0.00,0.00)
Plotting area is 204.98 wide by 277.45 high (MAX size)
Plot is NOT rotated 90 degrees
Hidden lines will NOT be removed
Scale is 10=1

Do you want to change anything? <N> Y
Write the plot to a file? <N>
Size units (Inches or Millimeters) <M>:
Plot origin in Millimeters <0.00,0.00>:

Standard values for plotting size

Size    Width   Height
MAX     204.98  277.45

Enter the Size or Width,Height (in Millimeters) <MAX>:
Rotate 2D plots 90 degrees clockwise? <N>
Remove hidden lines? <N>

Specify scale by entering:
Plotted Millimeters=Drawing Units or Fit or ? <10=1>:
```

Typical pre-plot screen.

Part Two
AutoCAD in Action

Creating Drawings

This part of the book shows you some practical sequences of AutoCAD commands and uses them to build up example drawings. Some of the exercises are based on simple shapes and buildings because their form is known to everyone and they therefore require the minimum of explanation. The wide range of techniques shown is easily applied to more technical drawings of mechanical components, electrical circuit boards and other specialities.

The drawings are created with step-by-step instructions but, in order to concentrate on the method, it is helpful if you already know basic AutoCAD routines. The prompt pages in Part One of the book explain the principal routines and you should experiment on screen, especially with the procedures for creating lines, arcs, circles; and for erasing them.

The step-by-step examples are not graded in order of difficulty of individual steps but the complexity of the drawings does build up and the explanations in the later exercises concentrate on new techniques.

When the instructions ask you to 'select' a certain AutoCAD command you are left to choose your own method of issuing that command because AutoCAD commands can be issued by a variety of methods. This book doesn't assume any particular layout for the menus at the side of the screen or the pull-down menus as they may be changed or customised on your version, or you may use a special menu on a tablet.

This diversity of methods for 'driving' AutoCAD is one of the strengths of the program. However, the AutoCAD command words used in the text do remain constant and a knowledge of them is needed if you eventually wish to create your own menus, icons and AutoLISP programs.

The best method for issuing a command is, like driving across London, to follow the route that you know. Try a mixture of side menus, pull-down menus and command words, depending on what you know and what seems closest to hand. You will develop a certain amount of cunning about the effects of different command routes. The pull-down menus, for example, generally leave the commands 'active', an effect which is sometimes helpful and sometimes a nuisance.

As with the commands, there are often several methods of building-up the same drawing on screen. Don't be paralysed by the sheer variety of these choices but also watch out for better methods such as shown in the example. Otherwise you may spend hours constructing objects using your own 'short-cuts' only to find that your entities are not versatile enough for later development.

Worksheet

This section is about an important drawing which at first does not seem to be a drawing at all. It is a *prototype* drawing which is stored for use as a blank 'worksheet' or 'style sheet' for other drawings. A prototype contains settings for units, layers and other items which suit your personal or office style of working.

You don't have to use a prototype but it is good practice and will therefore save you time. If you don't specify your own prototype drawing then AutoCAD loads a drawing screen based on its own prototype which is stored as the standard file called *acad.dwg*. The contents of the standard prototype supplied for European use include decimal units which are set up for A3/A4-sized paper.

AutoCAD commands and features which are used in this section include the following:

- LIMITS
- GRID
- SNAP
- COORDS
- UNITS
- LAYER
- PLINE
- LINE
- TEXT, DTEXT
- END

The techniques

The first sequence of activities takes you from the text of the Main Menu to the graphics of the Drawing Editor. You must invent a filename, such as *wksh1*, for the drawing. Remember that a filename must not be longer than 8 characters and must not contain spaces.

Your menu may offer SETUP options for setting paper size and hardcopy scale but these are not used here as they are offered again just before printout. A simple rule is to draw on screen in the 'real' units of the object and do the scaling at the printout stage. This worksheet will be useful for working in metres and other worksheets can be prepared for working in other units such as millimetres.

The edges of the drawing sheet are established with the LIMITS command and the settings of the GRID and SNAP commands are changed to suit the Limits. The setting of the UNITS command is made decimal with 3 digits after the decimal point.

The LAYER command is used to create separate layers for the border, and for the the text, dimensions and lines of future drawings. Layers can be given numbers but it is best to use names that explain themselves as it is possible, and often useful, to have dozens of layers. Colours are given to each layer and, even if you are viewing the layers in monochrome, these colours affect which pens are used in a plotter.

The border lines and text box are drawn on their own layer called 'border' and the current layer is then changed back to the '0' layer. The Freeze option is used to hide the border until the Thaw option is used in some future drawing. The 'dialogue boxes' in the pull-down menus of AutoCAD provide a convenient alternative of redefining layers.

Apart from the border there are no objects on this drawing but the worksheet contains plenty of information about units, scales and other settings. Before you save the worksheet with the END command, make sure that the settings are left as you wish to find them each time that you start a drawing.

Instructions

Follow the sequences of instructions listed under the 'Activity' columns and remember the following points:

- Commands can be 'selected' from menus or by typing command words.
- The layout of menus varies with your version of AutoCAD.
- Points can be 'picked' by pointing on screen and clicking, or by typing in coordinates.
- The prompt line at the bottom of the screen shows the current options.
- Use the **HELP** command or ? for on-screen information.
- Use **Ctrl-C** to cancel a wrong sequence and start again.
- The U for Undo command is useful for some mistakes.
- Boxes in the margin refer to a group of prompt pages in Part One of the book where commands are explained and illustrated.

Activity	Comment

See also
BASICS
Prompt pages

Activity	Comment
Select 1	to open drawing from Main Menu.
Enter *wksh1* [RETURN]	as filename for new drawing. The Main Menu text is replaced by the drawing screen.

	Activity	Comment
See also **UTILITIES** Prompt pages	Select **LIMITS** command	to set size of drawing area.
	[RETURN]	to accept 0, 0 for lower left corner.
	Enter 13, 9	to reset upper right corner
	Select **GRID** command	to change grid setting.
	Enter 1	as new spacing of grid. Ignore any messages about density of grid.
	Select **SNAP** command	to change snap setting.
	Enter 0.2	as new spacing of snap.
	Select **ZOOM** command	to change screen view
	Choose **All** option	to fill screen to limits.
	Set **GRID** to ON	use function key F7 on PCs.
	Set **SNAP** to ON	use function key F9 on PCs.
	Set **COORDS** to ON	use function key F6 on PCs.
	Select **LIMITS** command	to set size of drawing area.
	Enter [RETURN]	to accept 0, 0 for lower left corner.
	Enter 13, 9	to reset upper right corner.
	Select **UNITS** command	for drawing measurements.
	Choose **Decimal** option	
	Enter 3	to set number of digits to right of decimal point.

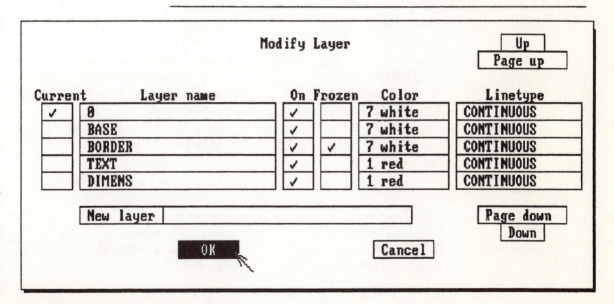

Modifying layers with pull-down menu.

Activity	Comment
Repeat [RETURN] as necessary	to accept standard values as settings of other settings.
Restore graphics screen if necessary	Use F1 key.
Select **LAYER** command	to create new layers.
Choose **New** option	to make layers.
Enter *base, border, text, dimens*	as names of new layers.
Choose Colour option	
Enter *white*	as choice of colour.
Enter *base, border*	as white layers.
Choose Colour option	
Enter *red*	as choice of colour.
Enter *text, dimens*	as red layers.
Choose **Set** option	to change current layer.
Enter *border*	as name of new current layer.
[RETURN]	Read top of screen to check that 'border' layer is current.

See also
ENTITIES
Prompt pages

Activity	Comment
Select **PLINE** command	to draw border.
Pick 0, 0	as start point.
pick 0, 9	as next point.
pick 13, 9	as next point.
pick 13, 0	as next point.
Choose **Close** option	to close figure.
Select **LINE** command	to draw text box.
Pick 11, 0	as start point.
Pick 11, 2	as next point.
Pick 13, 2	as next point.
[RETURN]	to complete command.
Set **SNAP** to OFF	use function key F9 on PCs.
Select **DTEXT** command	to write title.
Pick start point	for position of text.
Enter 0.2	as height of text.
Enter 0	as rotation angle.
	Or use [RETURN] to accept standard values.
Type *Your Name*	or suitable title.
Use [RETURN]	to start new lines.
[RETURN]	to complete command.
Repeat DTEXT or TEXT command	as desired.

Activity	Comment
Select **LAYER** command	to change layers.
Choose **Set** option	to request new current layer.
Enter 0	as name of new current layer.
Choose **Freeze** option	to hide border.
Enter *border*	as name of layer to freeze.
[RETURN]	border is made invisible.
Select **REDRAW** command	to clean screen marks.
Set **SNAP** to OFF	use function key F9 on PCs.
Select **END** command	to save current worksheet and exit to Main Menu.

See also
UTILITIES
Prompt pages

Layer BORDER   0.000,0.000

Yourname
Project

Screen view of blank worksheet with grid set on.

Further activities

Create other worksheet prototypes which suit your own drawing habits.
The following settings may be useful:

- *wksh100* with upper right limit of 1300, 900. Useful for objects
  dimensioned in centimetres.
- *wksh1000* with upper right limit of 13000, 9000. Useful for buildings
  dimensioned in millimetres.

The standard prototype drawing, which AutoCAD uses until you change
it, is usually set with an upper right limit of 420, 297. This setting
corresponds to the dimensions, in mm, of A3 paper.

If you rename one of your own prototype drawings as *acad.dwg* then it
will become the automatic drawing sheet loaded by AutoCAD.

Simple Shapes

The aim of this section is to use a wide selection of AutoCAD drawing and editing tools. The shapes drawn are not as important as the techniques used; your results will not be saved for posterity!

Although the drawings look simple, the exercises may force you to explore AutoCAD features that you haven't used before. All the techniques will bring rewards of efficiency in your later drawing and it is useful to practise them now.

AutoCAD commands and features which are used in this section include the following:

- GRID
- SNAP
- COORDS
- LINE
- ARC
- TRIM
- FILLET
- REDRAW

- ZOOM
- OSNAP
- CHANGE
- ERASE
- MIRROR
- ARRAY
- QUIT

The techniques

The first sequence of activities takes you from the main text menu of AutoCAD to the drawing editor. The new filename, such as *blade*, is linked to that of the prototype previously saved as *wksh1*. When the new drawing screen appears it already contains the limits, units and other setting of the standard worksheet.

To keep the example simple and uncluttered, the instructions assume that your screen is about 13 drawing units wide and 9 units high. If necessary, use the LIMITS command as shown in the *Worksheet* instruction. Otherwise, use whatever units are on screen and just follow the general shapes of the sample drawings and draw them to occupy most of the screen.

It is just *not* possible to locate or to join lines accurately by using your hand and eye – magnification with the ZOOM command will soon show that there is always a gap! For these drawing exercises, as for most real drawings, you need to enter the actual measurements or to use the drawing aids. The sequences show the use of the GRID and SNAP settings and the second drawing uses the more powerful OSNAP (Object Snap) setting to locate points.

The *Blade* shape is first drawn as a simple outline with the LINE and ARC commands. The ERASE command is used to remove the unwanted diagonal line and the TRIM command is used to cut the indent in the top right corner. The FILLET command is used to convert the right-angled corner to a curve.

The *Cogwheel* drawing uses an outer circle and vertical line as temporary markers to help draw the sloping line of the top cog. The CHANGE command is used to trim the sloping line and the MIRROR command makes a reverse image of the line. The ERASE command rubs out the temporary markers and the ARRAY command automatically generates a pattern of cogs around the circle.

Instructions

Follow the sequences of instructions listed under the 'Activity' columns and remember the following points:

- Commands can be 'selected' from menus or by typing command words.
- The layout of menus varies with your version of AutoCAD.
- Points can be 'picked' by pointing on screen and clicking, or by typing in coordinates.
- The prompt line at the bottom of the screen shows the current options.
- Use the **HELP** command or ? for on-screen information.
- Use **Ctrl-C** to cancel a wrong sequence and start again.
- The U for Undo command is useful for some mistakes.
- Boxes in the margin refer to a group of prompt pages in Part One of the book where commands are explained and illustrated.

Blade

Activity	Comment
Select 1	to open drawing from Main Menu.
Enter *Blade=wksh1*	to start new drawing file with same settings as worksheet.
Set **GRID** to ON	use function key F7 on PCs.
Set **SNAP** to ON	use function key F9 on PCs.

See also
BASICS
Prompt pages

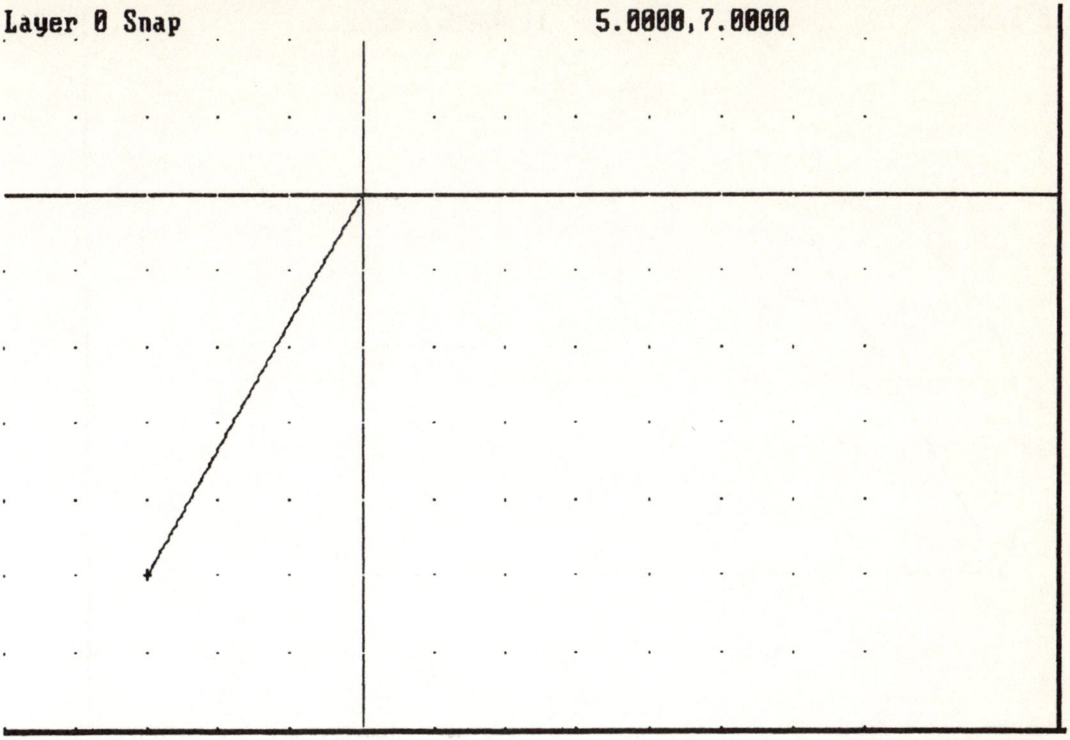

Layer 0 Snap   5.0000,7.0000

End point of first line being picked by cursor.
Coordinates display set on.

Activity	Comment
Set **COORDS** to ON	use function key F6 on PCs.
Select **LINE** command	to draw initial outline.
Pick 2, 2	as first point (from).
Pick 5, 7	as second point.
Reset **COORDS** if necessary.	use function key F6 on PCs.
Pick 11, 7	as third point.
Pick 11, 2	as fourth point.
Choose **Close** option	to close figure.
Select **ARC** command	to draw curved left end.
Choose **3-point** option	
Pick 2, 2	as first point.
Pick 2, 5	as second point.
Pick 5, 7	as end point.
Select **LINE** command	to draw indent at top right.
Pick 9, 7	as first point.
Pick 9, 5	as second point.

See also
ENTITIES
Prompt pages

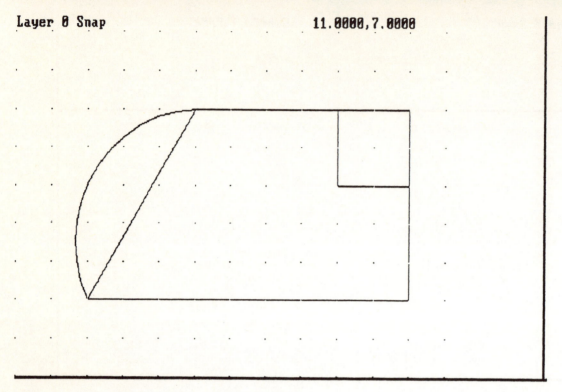

Layer 0 Snap   11.0000,7.0000

Initial shape formed by LINE and ARC commands.

Activity	Comment
Pick 11, 5	as third point.
[RETURN]	to complete command.
Set **SNAP** to OFF	use function key F9 on PCs.
Select **ERASE** command	to remove unwanted diagonal line at left end.
Pick any point on diagonal line	as first selected object.
[RETURN]	to complete command.
Set **SNAP** to ON	use function key F9 on PCs.
Select **TRIM** command	to remove top right corner.
Pick 9, 6	as cutting edge.
Pick 10, 5	as second cutting edge.
[RETURN]	
Pick 10, 7	as object to trim.
Pick 11, 6	as second object to trim.
[RETURN]	
Select **FILLET** command	to change inside corner to a curve.

See also
CHANGES
Prompt pages

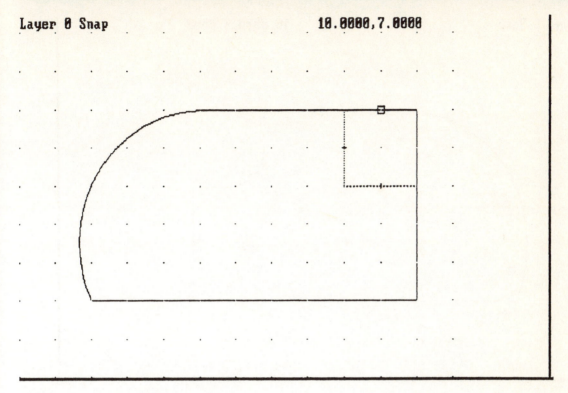

Layer 0 Snap   10.0000,7.0000

Indent being cut with TRIM command.

Activity	Comment
Choose **Radius** option	
Enter 1	as radius of corner.
Pick 9, 6	on first object.
Pick 10, 5	on second object.
Select **REDRAW** command	to clean screen marks.
Select **QUIT** command	to leave drawing.
Enter Y	to agree to abandon drawing and return to Main Menu.

Cogwheel

Activity	Comment
Select 1	to open drawing from Main Menu.

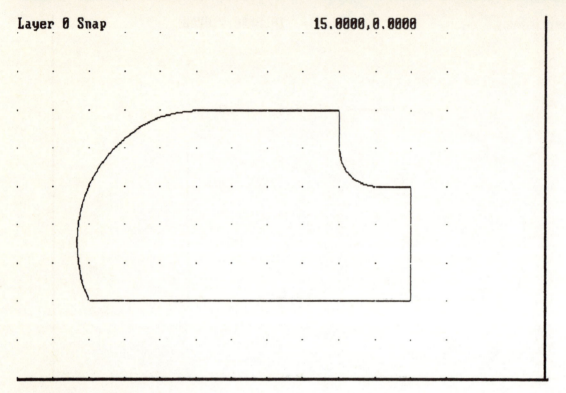

Layer 0 Snap   15.0000,0.0000

Final shape of Blade *sequence.*

Activity	Comment
Enter *cogwheel=wksh1*	to start new drawing file with same settings as worksheet.
Set **GRID** to ON	use function key F7 on PCs.
Set **SNAP** to ON	use function key F9 on PCs.
Set **COORDS** to ON	use function key F6 on PCs.
Select **CIRCLE** command	to draw inner circle.
Choose **CEN,RAD** option	
Pick 6, 5 near centre of screen	as centre of circle.
Enter 2, or drag point	to give radius of 2.
Select **OFFSET** command	to produce outer circle.
Enter 0.4	as offset distance.
Pick point on circle	as object to offset.
Pick any point outside circle	as side to offset.
[RETURN]	to complete command.
Select **LINE** command	to draw short vertical reference line.
Pick 6, 8	as first point.

See also
ENTITIES
Prompt pages

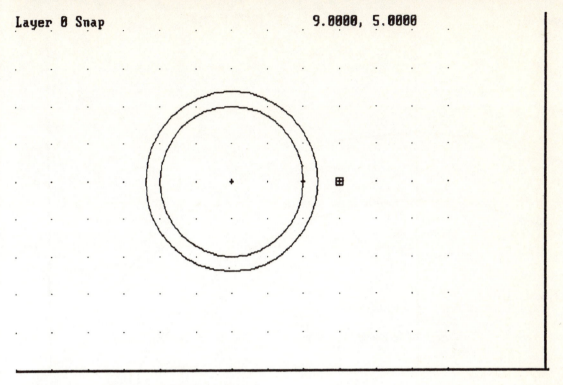

Layer 0 Snap   9.0000, 5.0000

Outer circle created by OFFSET command.

Activity	Comment
Pick 6, 6	as second point.
[RETURN]	to complete command.
Set **SNAP** to OFF	use function key F9 on PCs.
Select **ZOOM** command	to magnify view of top part of drawing.
Choose **Window** option	
Pick near 5, 8	as first corner of window.
Pick near 7, 6	as other corner of window.
Select **LINE** command	to draw sloping line.
Activate **OSNAP**	use **** at top of menu.
Choose **INTERsect** option	from OSNAP menu.
Pick 6, 7.4	with help of OSNAP target.
Enter @0.6<240	as relative distance and angle to next point.
[RETURN]	
Select **CHANGE** command	to shorten last line.
Choose **Last** option	to select line.

See also
UTILITIES
Prompt pages

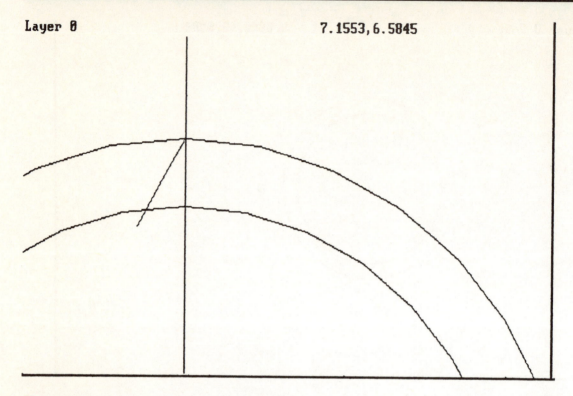

Layer 0   7.1553,6.5845

First side of cog before trimming and MIRROR command.

Activity	Comment
[RETURN]	
Activate **OSNAP**	use **** at top of menu.
Choose **INTERsect** option	from OSNAP menu.
Pick intersection of last line and inner circle	with help of OSNAP target.
Select **REDRAW** command	to clean marks from screen.
Set **SNAP** to ON	use function key F9 on PCs.
Select **MIRROR** command	to duplicate last line.
Choose **Last** option	to select line.
[RETURN]	
Pick 6, 8	as first point of mirror line.
Pick 6, 7	as second point of mirror line.
[RETURN]	to keep old object.
Set **SNAP** to OFF	use function key F9 on PCs.
Select **ERASE** command	to remove temporary markers.
Pick vertical line	at any point.
Pick outer circle	at any point.
[RETURN]	

See also
CHANGES
Prompt pages

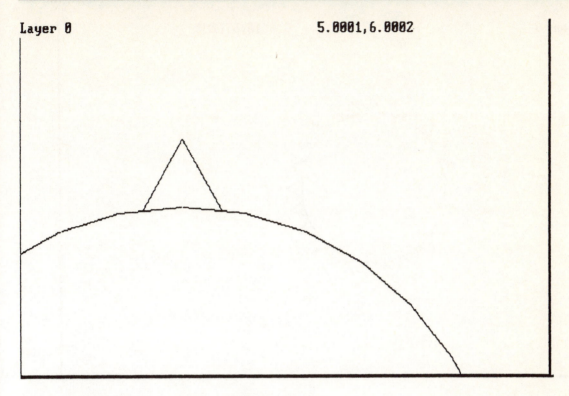

Layer 0   5.0001,6.0002

Single cog before multiplication by ARRAY command.

Activity	Comment
Select **ARRAY** command	to generate a pattern of cogs.
Pick left sloping line	as first selected object.
Pick right sloping line	as second selected object.
[RETURN]	
Choose **Polar** option	to produce circular array.
Activate **OSNAP**	use **** at top of menu.
Choose **CENter** option	from OSNAP menu.
Pick any point on circle	as object with centre.
Enter 24	as number of items.
[RETURN]	to accept 360 degrees.
[RETURN]	to rotate objects.
Select **ZOOM** command	to view complete drawing.
Choose **Previous** option	to return original view.
Select **QUIT** command	to leave drawing.
Enter *Y*	to agree to abandon drawing and return to Main Menu.

See also
OUTPUTS
Prompt pages

Layer 0   8.6218,5.6090

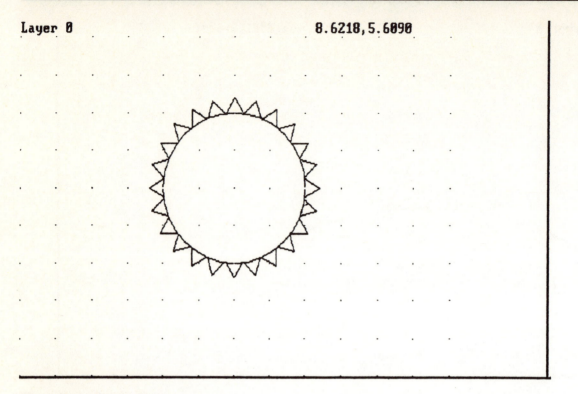

Final shape of Cogwheel *sequence.*

Further activities

Draw shapes of your own choice and make use of the commands and sequences used in the above examples. In particular, try other options of the ARC command to create linked arcs and lines. Consult the prompt pages in the first section of the book to get more details about commands.

The final illustrations show an orthographic (multi-view) drawing of a nut. The construction lines and circles are drawn on a separate layer which is frozen before the final plot. The OSNAP mode is useful for attaching lines and arcs to intersections of construction lines. The POLYGON command is one method of drawing the hexagonal sides of the nut.

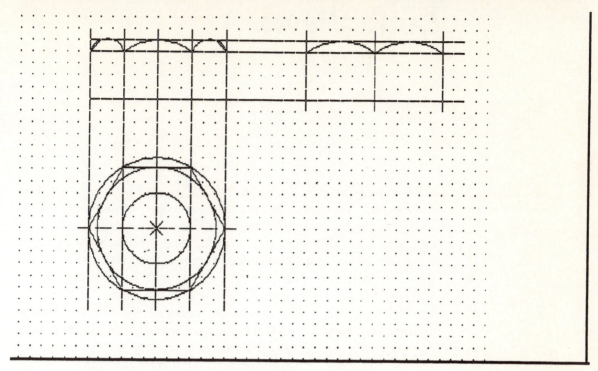

Formation of nut drawing using construction lines.

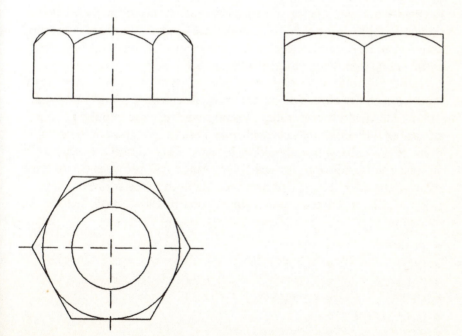

Completed nut drawing with construction layer frozen.

Solid Views

Solid objects exist in three dimensions yet drawings are only two-dimensional. Draughting has therefore developed various conventions, such as orthographic and isometric projections, for showing solid detail on paper. AutoCAD allows you to produce any of these views and there are drawings aids to help you, such as changing coordinate systems and the ISOPLANE command.

AutoCAD offers the extra possibility of transforming a 2D drawing into 3D with just a few commands, provided that there is enough information about the third dimension. Some objects can be given a relatively fast and satisfying 3D effect but a structure like a building, even a simple shed, requires the planning shown in later examples.

Another consideration is whether you are drawing 'real' solid shapes or 'visualisations' of solid shapes. For example, if you wish to use your drawing information to communicate with a machine then all the 3D information about shapes and surfaces must be accurate. Construction drawings, on the other hand, communicate to the eye and are concerned with accurate appearances and dimensions. Both approaches to constructing a drawing have their complexities.

AutoCAD offers several methods of 'jumping' into the third dimension. A drawing of a box, for example, can be 'extruded' into space to look like a wire-frame cube. This approach is good enough for many effects but difficulties may start when you ask the program to 'hide' those parts of the cube which shouldn't be seen. This section introduces the various commands and options which AutoCAD provides for treating solids and a later section demonstrates methods of visualisation.

AutoCAD commands and features used in this section include the following:

- PLINE
- LINE
- ARRAY
- COPY
- CHAMFER
- ZOOM
- 3DFACE
- VPOINT
- HIDE
- SOLID
- ELEV
- UCS
- UCSICON
- RULESURF

The technique

When you draw an object in just two dimensions AutoCAD automatically leaves the extruded 'height' at zero. You won't miss the height unless you try to view your object in 3D – it will then appear flat! The extruded *thickness* (height) of the object can be set by the SETVAR (THICKNESS) command (Earlier versions of the program used the ELEV command).

AutoCAD also allows you to add a third dimension (the z-coordinate) at the time that you specify each point of an object. The z-coordinate can also be entered in relevant editing commands such as those for used for copying or moving. When no z-coordinate is specified, as when using a pointer, the previous setting is used for all subsequent points. Fortunately the CHANGE command enables you to go back and reset the thickness, or any other properties, of an object. The MOVE command can also be used to change the position of the construction plane (elevation).

All coordinate points are measured as distances from the origin point of the coordinate system. The preferred method for setting construction planes is to use an origin and axes which are related to the object you are drawing. The UCS command sets and controls this *User Coordinate System*, as shown in the final sequences of this section.

Table

In the first set of drawing sequences, a simple table is created with 4 circular legs and a rectangular top. The corners of the top are then chamfered. The CIRCLE command is used to draw one table leg and the ARRAY command then generates copies of this object in a controlled pattern. The outline of the table top is drawn as a single entity with the PLINE command and the corners are then angled with the CHAMFER command.

The VPOINT command gives a 3D view constructed with parallel projection (use DVIEW for perspective projections). You can accurately specify the 3D viewing position by entering the 3 coordinates (x, y, z). AutoCAD also offers more visual methods of setting viewpoint such as rotating the axes on screen, moving a point over a spherical surface, or choosing from a menu of viewpoint directions.

The HIDE command changes the 'wire-frame' appearance of the table legs into a solid-looking objects. The table top appears to be made of glass but this is because the simple polyline used for the table top does not behave as a horizontal 3D surface. To produce an opaque table top you can use a polyline with width, a 3D Face or other solids, as shown next.

Sofa

The second set of sequences creates a simple sofa shape which gives a better 3D visualisation. The back and sides of the sofa are drawn using the width option of the PLINE command. Notice that the end points of a wide polyline occur on the centre line. The SOLID command is used to draw the seating area of the sofa.

Cubetube

The final set of instructions, entitled 'cubetube', demonstrates the User Coordinate System and some of the AutoCAD 3D commands. The 3DFACE and COPY commands are used to construct all faces of the cube. Notice that 3D faces can be copied like any other entity. The UCS command is re-aligned with one face of the cube to allow a circle to be accurately drawn upon that face. Instead of extruding the circle with a thickness, the RULESURF command is used to create a ruled line 3D surface between two circles.

AutoCAD has other special commands – TABSURF, REVSURF and EDGESURF – which simplify the creation of 3D surfaces.

The END command stores the drawings as files on the computer disk. Drawing files are usually kept in their own storage area and the filename must be preceded by the appropriate name of the drive letter or subdirectory. For example: *B:table* will store the file on floppy disk B: and *work*\table will store the file in a subdirectory called 'work'.

Instructions

Follow the sequences of instructions listed under the 'Activity' columns and remember the following points.

- Commands can be 'selected' from menus or by typing command words.
- The layout of menus can vary with your version of AutoCAD.
- Points can be 'picked' by pointing on screen and clicking, or by typing in coordinates.
- The prompt line at the bottom of the screen shows the current options.
- Use the **HELP** command or **?** for on-screen information.
- Use **Ctrl-C** to cancel a wrong sequence and start again.
- The U for Undo command is useful for some mistakes.
- Boxes in the margin refer to a group of prompt pages in Part One of the book where commands are explained and illustrated.

Table

Activity	Comment
Select 1	to open drawing from Main Menu.
Enter *table=wksh1*	to start new drawing file with same settings as worksheet.
Set **GRID** to ON	use function key F7 on PCs.
Set **SNAP** to ON	use function key F9 on PCs.
Set **COORDS** to ON	use function key F6 on PCs.
Select **ELEV** command	to set 3D level and thickness of table legs (or use **CHANGE** command).
Enter 0	for new current elevation (construction plane).
Enter 2	for new current thickness (height).
Select **CIRCLE** command	to draw table leg.

See also
UTILITIES
Prompt pages

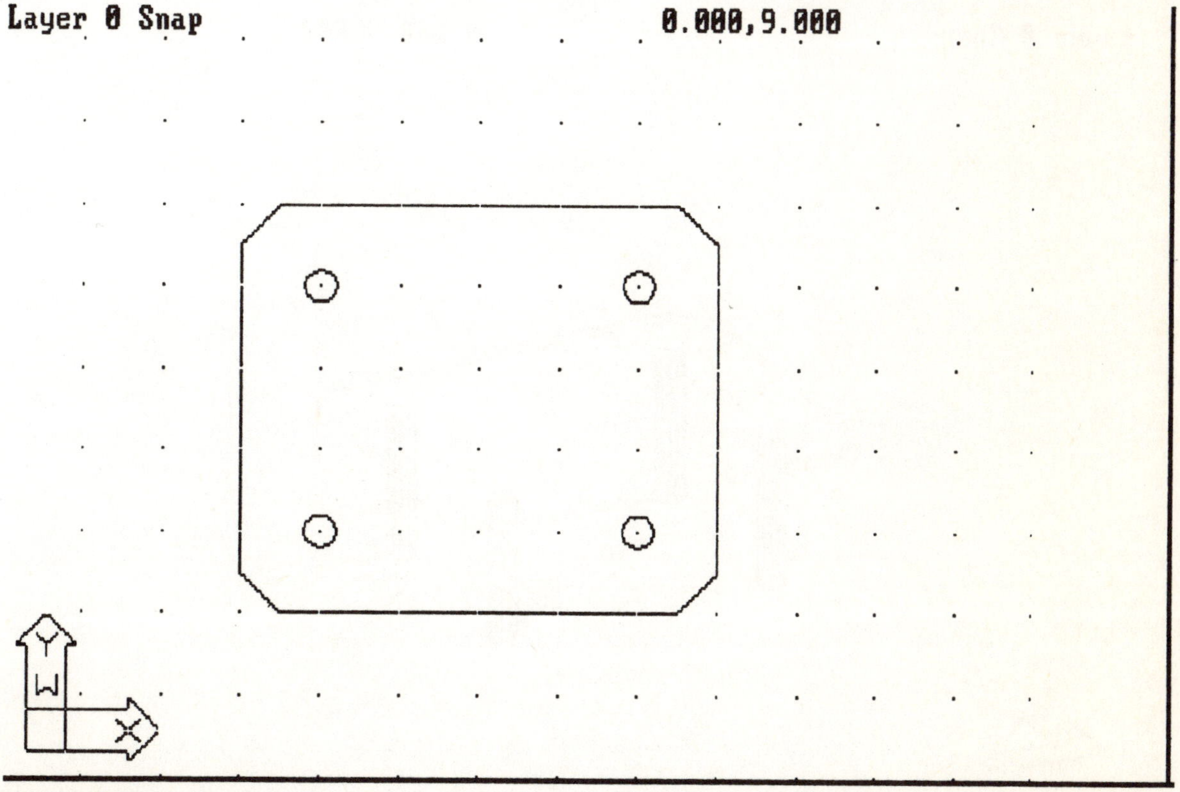

Layer 0 Snap   0.000,9.000

Table components in 2D.

Activity	Comment
Choose **Centre, Radius** option	
Pick 4, 3	as centre point.
Enter 0.2	as radius.
Select **ARRAY** command	to generate pattern.
Choose **Last** option	to select object.
[RETURN]	to complete selection.
Choose **Rectangular** option	for type of the array.
Enter 2	as number of rows.
Enter 2	as number of columns.
Enter 3	as distance between rows.
Enter 4	as distance between columns.
Select **ELEV** command	to set 3D level and thickness.
	for table top (or use **CHANGE** command).
Enter 2	for new current elevation.
Enter 0.1	for new current thickness height.

See also
CHANGES
Prompt pages

Layer 0 Snap   **0.000,9.000**

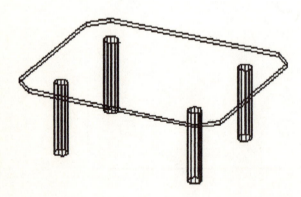

Effect of VPOINT and HIDE commands.

Activity	Comment
Select **PLINE** command	to draw table top.
Pick 3, 2	as first point.
Pick 3, 7	as endpoint.
Pick 9, 7	as next endpoint.
Pick 9, 2	as next endpoint.
Choose **Close** option	to complete polyline.
Select **CHAMFER** command	to trim corners.
Choose **Distances** option	
Enter 0.5	as first chamfer distance.
[RETURN]	for second chamfer distance.
Choose **Polyline** option	
Pick anywhere on rectangle	use target to select object.
	The 4 corners should become chamfered.
Select **VPOINT** command	to start 3D view.
[RETURN]	

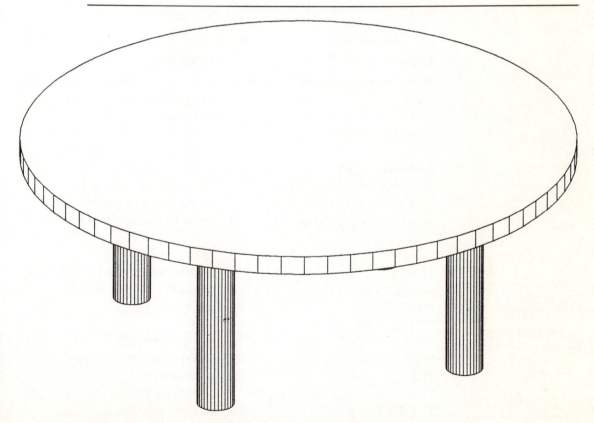

Effect of HIDE command on circular table top.

Activity	Comment

See also
OUTPUTS
Prompt pages

Activity	Comment
Enter 1, –2, 1	as viewpoint coordinates, or use screen viewpoint system.
Select **HIDE** command	
Choose **Yes** option	to remove hidden lines.
	Table is shown as 3D visualisation. Top is not treated as solid.
Select **VPOINT** command	to restore 2D view.
Enter 0, 0, 1	as viewpoint,
	or choose Plan option.
Select **ZOOM** command	to see complete drawing sheet.
Choose **All** option	
Select **END** command	to save drawing and return to Main Menu.

Sofa

Activity	Comment
Select 1	to open drawing from Main Menu.
Enter *table=wksh1*	to start new drawing file with same settings as worksheet.
Set **GRID** to ON	or use function key F7.
Set **SNAP** to ON	or use function key F9.
Set **COORDS** to ON	or use function key F6.
Select **ELEV** command	to set level and height for 3D view.
Enter 0	as new current elevation.
Enter 4	as new current thickness (height).
Select **PLINE** command	to draw sofa back and sides.
Pick 2, 2	as first point.
Choose **width** option	
Enter 2	as starting width.
[RETURN]	to keep ending width as 2.
Pick 2, 6	as endpoint.
Pick 12, 6	as next endpoint.
Pick 12, 2	as next endpoint.
Select **FILL OFF**	

See also
ENTITIES
Prompt pages

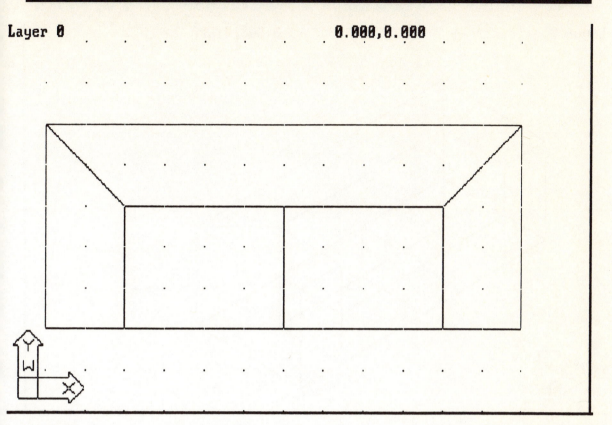

Layer 0   0.000,0.000

Sofa outline in 2D.

Activity	Comment
[RETURN]	to complete command.
Select **ELEV** command	to set 3D level and height for reminder of sofa.
[RETURN]	to keep current elevation 0.
Enter 2	as new current thickness.
Select **SOLID** command	to draw middle of sofa.
Pick 3, 5	as first point.
Pick 7, 5	as second point.
Pick 3, 2	as third point.
Pick 7, 2	as fourth point.
[RETURN]	to complete command.
[RETURN]	to repeat SOLID command.
Pick 7, 5	as first point.
Pick 11, 5	as second point.
Pick 7, 2	as third point.
Pick 11, 1	as fourth point.

Layer 0   0.000,0.000

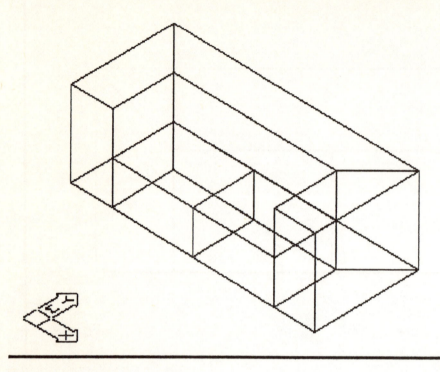

Effect of VPOINT command.

	Activity	Comment
	[RETURN]	
See also **OUTPUTS** Prompt pages	Select **VPOINT** command	to start 3D view.
	[RETURN]	
	Enter 1,–1,1	as viewpoint.
		or use axes display on screen.
	Select **HIDE** command	
	Choose **Yes** option	to remove hidden lines.
		Sofa is shown as 3D visualisation with solid surfaces.
	Select **VPOINT** command	to return to 2D view.
	Enter 0, 0, 1	as viewpoint.
		or choose plan option.
	Select **ZOOM** command	to see complete drawing sheet.
	Choose **All** option	
	Select **END** command	to save drawing and return to Main Menu.

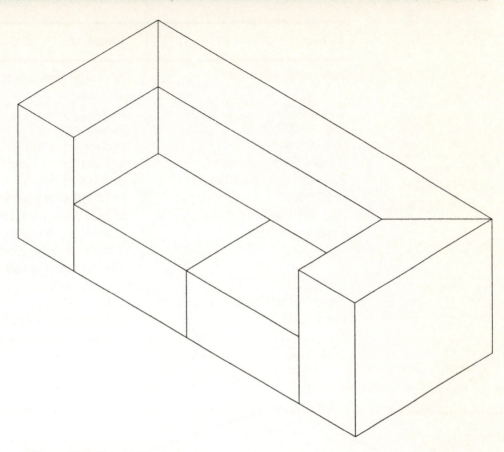

Effect of HIDE command.

Cubetube

Activity	Comment
Select 1	to open drawing from Main Menu.
Enter *cubetube*	to start new drawing file using standard AutoCAD settings.
Set **SNAP** to ON	use function key F9 on PCs.
Set **GRID** to ON	use function key F7 on PCs.
Set **ORTHO** to ON	use function key F8 on PCs.
Select **3DFACE** command	to draw base of cube.
Pick 100, 50	as first point.
	Or use any suitable points on your screen to give square outline.

See also
ENTITIES
Prompt pages

Activity	Comment
Pick @200, 0	as relative coordinate for second point.
Pick @0, 200	as third point.
Pick @–200, 0	as fourth point.
[RETURN]	to complete command.
Select **COPY** command	to form top of cube.
Pick any part of outline	to select object.
[RETURN]	to complete selection.
Pick any corner of outline	as base point for COPY.
Enter @0, 0, 100	as relative 3D distance for second point of displacement.
	The 2D drawing will seem unchanged.
Select **VPOINT** command	to start 3D view.
Enter 3, –3, 2	as viewpoint coordinates.
	Or use screen viewpoint systems.

See also
CHANGES
Prompt pages

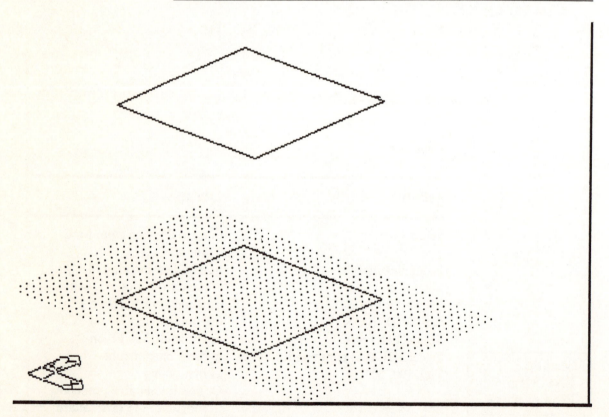

Bottom and top of cube after VPOINT command.

Activity	Comment
Set **SNAP** to OFF	use function key F9 on PCs.
Select **OSNAP** command	to set object attachment.
Choose **INTersection** option	to identify corner points during following commands.
Select **3DFACE** command	to draw front face of cube.
Pick following points on screen with help of OSNAP target box:	
Pick 100, 50	as first point.
Pick 300, 50	as second point.
Pick 300, 50, 200	as third point, with z-height.
Pick 100, 50, 200	as fourth point, with z-height.
[RETURN]	to complete command.
Select **COPY** command	to form back face of cube.
Pick any point on upright edge of front face	to select object.

See also
UTILITIES
Prompt pages

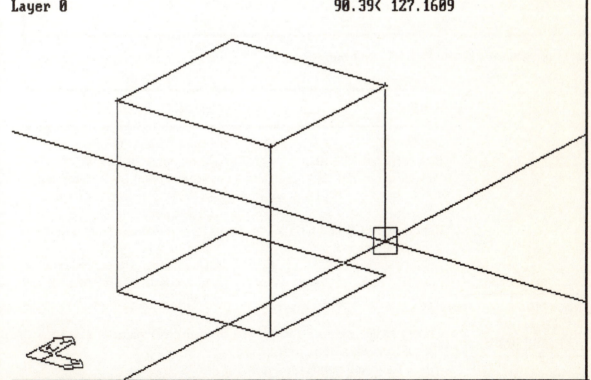

Layer 0   90.39⟨ 127.1609

Drawing side face with 3DFACE command.

Layer 0 Ortho   551.94,-122.46

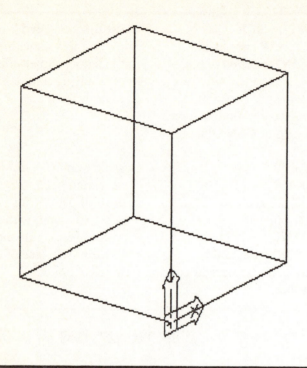

Change of coordinate system by UCS command.

Activity	Comment
[RETURN]	to complete selection.
Pick corner at 100, 50, 0	as base point for COPY.
Pick corner at 100, 250	as second point of displacement.
	Use OSNAP target box to pick above points.
Repeat **3DFACE** and **COPY** procedures	to form remaining front and back face of cube.
	All six faces of the cube should now consist of 3DFACES.
Select **UCS** command	to define User Coordinate System.
Choose **3point** option	to define XY plane of new UCS.
Use OSNAP target box to help pick following points on screen:	
Pick 300, 50, 0	as new origin point.
Pick 300, 250, 0	as point on X-axis.

See also
UTILITIES
Prompt pages

Activity	Comment
Pick 300, 50, 200	as point on Y-axis.
Select **OSNAP** command	to change object attachment.
[RETURN]	to give null setting.
Select **CIRCLE** command	
Choose **Centre/Radius** option	
Enter 100, 100	as centre of cube face using new current coordinate system.
Enter 50	as radius.
Select **COPY** command	to duplicate circle.
Pick any point on circle	to select object.
[RETURN]	to complete selection.
Activate **OSNAP**	use **** at top of menu.
Select Centre option	
Pick any point on circle	to allow OSNAP to find centre of circle as base point for COPY.

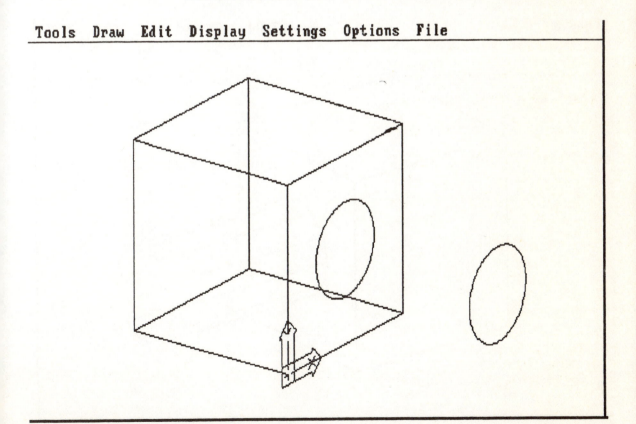

Tools   Draw   Edit   Display   Settings   Options   File

Circles produced by CIRCLE and COPY commands.

Activity	Comment
Enter @0, 0, 100	as second point of displacement using relative current coordinates.
Select **RULESURF** command	to create 3D surface between two circles.
Pick first circle	as first defining curve.
Pick second circle	as second defining curve.
Select **UCS** command	
Choose **previous** option	to restore original User Coordinate System.
Select **UCSICON**	to change onscreen coordinate icon.
Choose Off option	to hide icon.
Select **HIDE** command	to remove hidden lines from current viewpoint.

See also
ENTITIES
Prompt pages

Layer 0   62.84,   899.44

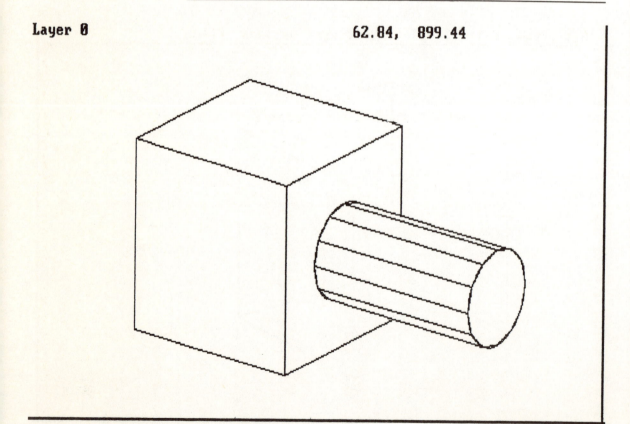

Effect of RULESURF and HIDE commands.

Activity	Comment
Select **END** command	to save drawing and return to Main Menu.

Further practice

Recall one of the drawings and experiment with different viewpoints. Try the effects of viewpoint coordinates (1, 1, 1); (1, 1, –1); (1, –1, 1) and so forth. Make a note of the coordinates for any viewpoints which may find useful.

The final illustration of the 'cubetube' example shows a split screen which is obtained with the VPORTS command, explained in a later section.

Layer 0   −14.41, 268.25

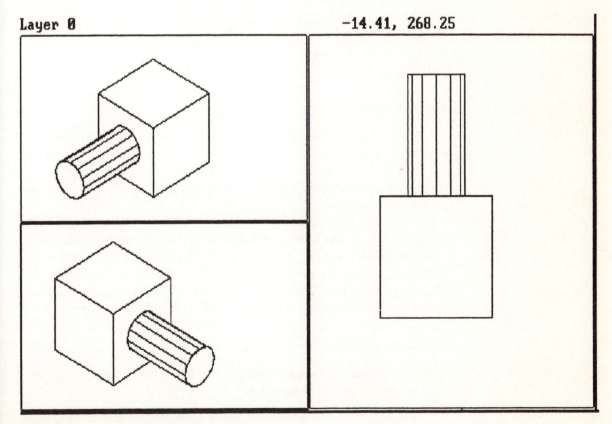

Multiple views using VPORTS command.

Dimensions and Patterns

AutoCAD allows you to automatically place dimensions on any part of a drawing or to fill areas with a variety of patterns. Although we view drawings as images on a screen, AutoCAD always thinks in the form of numbers and therefore can easily produce numerical details, such as dimensions, about any part of a drawing.

Areas of a drawing can be filled-in with patterns or 'crosshatches'. AutoCAD offers a range of automatic fill patterns, including many of those used as standards in the engineering and construction industries.

AutoCAD commands and features used in this section include the following:

- DIM
- OSNAP
- REDRAW
- HATCH
- UNDO
- END
- QUIT

The techniques

The first exercise adds dimensions to the previous drawing called *blade* but any drawing with some variety of shape can be used. The various options of the DIM command are used to place the dimensions around the sides of the shape. The OSNAP setting is used to locate the midpoint of the arc for the radius option.

The second exercise uses the previously-saved drawing called *table* but any similar shape can be used. The 2D 'table top' might be thought of as a plate with four bolt holes. Initially the HATCH command totally fills the figure with pattern, including the holes so the UNDO command is used to clear the pattern. The Window option of the HATCH command is one of several methods of getting a pattern which does not fill the holes.

Instructions

Follow the sequences of instructions listed under the 'Activity' columns and remember the following points:

- Commands can be 'selected' from menus or by typing command words.

- The layout of menus varies with your version of AutoCAD.
- Points can be 'picked' by pointing on screen and clicking, or by typing in coordinates.
- The prompt line at the bottom of the screen shows the current options.
- Use the **HELP** command or **?** for on-screen information.
- Use **Ctrl-C** to cancel a wrong sequence and start again.
- The **U** for Undo command is useful for some mistakes.
- Boxes in the margin refer to a group of prompt pages in Part One of the book where commands are explained and illustrated.

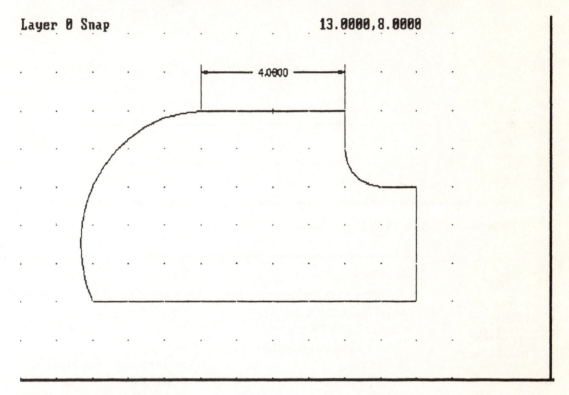

Initial horizontal dimension.

Dimensioning

Activity	Comment
Select 1	from Main Menu.
Enter *dimen=blade*	to start new drawing based on existing drawing of blade.
	Or use similar simple shape.

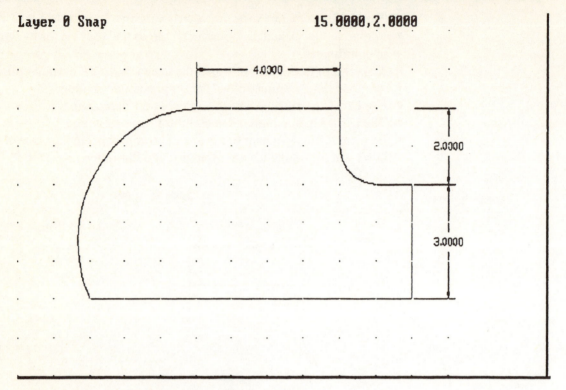

Layer 0 Snap   15.0000,2.0000

4.0000

2.0000

3.0000

Vertical dimension with Continue option.

Activity	Comment
Select **DIM** command	
Choose **LINEAR** option	
Choose **Horizontal** option	
[RETURN]	to choose selection option.
Pick 7, 7 or similar	to select top line.
Pick 7, 8 or similar	as dimension line location.
[RETURN]	to accept dimension text.
	Dim command remains current.
Choose **Vertical** option	
Pick 11, 7	as first extension line origin.
Pick 11, 5	as second extension line origin.
Pick 12, 6	as dimension line location.
[RETURN]	to accept dimension text.
	Dim command remains current.
Choose **Continue** option	
Pick 11, 2	as second extension line origin.
[RETURN]	to accept dimension text.
	Dim command remains current.

See also
ENTITIES
Prompt pages

Activity	Comment
Choose **Horizontal** option	
[RETURN]	to choose selection option.
Pick 7, 2 or similar	to select bottom line.
Pick 7, 1 or similar	as dimension line location.
[RETURN]	to accept dimension text. Dim command remains current.
Choose **Aligned** option	
Pick 2, 2	as first extension line origin.
Pick 5, 7	as second extension line origin.
Pick 2, 6	as dimension line location.
[RETURN]	to accept dimension text.
Set **SNAP** to OFF	use function key F9 on PCs. Dim command remains current.
Choose **Radius** option	
Activate **OSNAP**	use **** at top of menu.
Choose **MIDpoint** option	from OSNAP menu. Dim command remains current.
Pick point on left arc	with help of OSNAP menu.

See also
UTILITIES
Prompt pages

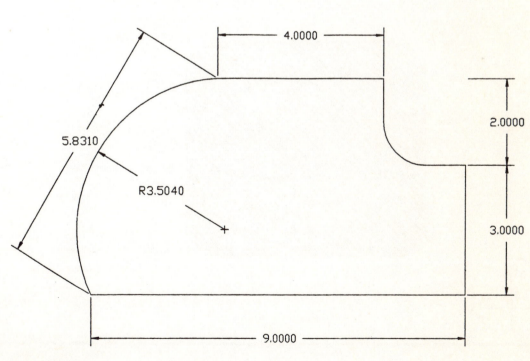

Final drawing.

Activity	Comment
[RETURN]	to accept dimension text.
Select **REDRAW** command	to clean screen marks.
Select **END** command	to save current drawing and return to Main Menu.

Hatching

Activity	Comment
Select 2	from Main Menu.
Enter *table*	to edit existing drawing.
	Or use similar simple shape.
Set **SNAP** to OFF	use function key F9 on PCs.

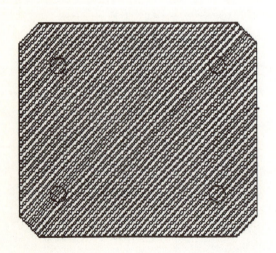

Initial effect of HATCH command.

Activity	Comment
Select **HATCH** command	to fill shape with pattern.
Choose **?** option	to see list of hatch patterns.
[RETURN]	
[RETURN]	to repeat HATCH command.
Enter *steel* or other choice	as name of pattern.
[RETURN]	to keep standard scale.
[RETURN]	to keep standard angle.
Pick any edge of outline	to select objects.
[RETURN]	to complete selection.
	Hatch pattern completely fills shape, including holes.
Select **U** command	to undo last command.
[RETURN]	to clear hatch pattern.
Select **HATCH** pattern	to selectively hatch areas.
Enter *Steel* or other choice	as name of pattern.
[RETURN]	to keep standard scale.
[RETURN]	to keep standard angle.
Choose **Window** option	
Pick first and second corners of window	to include all objects on screen.
[RETURN]	to complete selection.
	Hatch pattern fills shape but avoids holes.
Select **QUIT** command	to return to Main Menu without saving work.
Enter *Y*	to confirm quit.

See also
ENTITIES
Prompt pages

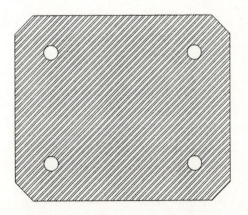

Selective use of HATCH command.

Further activities

Experiment with the other options of the DIM command, such as those for marking the size of angles and for changing the size of the dimension text.

Choose other types of standard hatch pattern and experiment by changing the size and rotation of these patterns. You can also create your own hatch patterns as explained in Part Three.

Building Shell

The aim of this section is to produce the outline of a simple building and to meet techniques which apply to drawing any subject. For the moment the building can be imagined as the shell of a holiday cabin. Later it can be multiplied into sets of cabins or even grouped into apartments.

If you find that you often do similar AutoCAD sequences, such as drawing parallel sides of walls or pipes, then the process can usually be automated using the AutoLISP programming language. It is common to buy ready-made packages of drawing routines. For example, Autodesk's own AEC architectural add-on for AutoCAD makes easy work of many tasks such as drawing cavity walls and closing the edges (reveals) when you make a break in a wall.

AutoCAD commands and features used in this section include the following:

- ORTHO
- LAYER
- LINE
- OFFSET
- FILLET
- COPY
- BREAK
- OSNAP
- ZOOM
- PAN
- REDRAW
- PRPLOT (PRINTER)

The techniques

The first sequence of activities takes you from the Main Menu of AutoCAD to the drawing editor. The filename *cabin1* is linked to the prototype previously saved as *wksh1*. In addition to your standard settings the prototype drawing contains the pre-prepared border and title box of the standard worksheet on a 'frozen' layer which must be thawed.

For this drawing, the units at the top of the drawing screen can be used to mean metres and decimals of a metre. The coordinates used for the outer edges of this building shell are convenient whole numbers which coincide with the snap grid. Real-life coordinates usually have to be given in the form of relative distances, such as those used here for some of the door openings.

You should turn SNAP and other aids on, or off again, depending on the drawing task. Although helpful, the snap effect can prevent you picking some points. The SNAP command can be used to change the setting of the snap effect, otherwise it remains at the setting contained in the *worksheet* prototype.

The ORTHO setting is a drawing aid which forces all lines to be either vertical or horizontal and you will see the effect on your cursor. Like snap, the ortho effect is useful when you want it but can be obstructive when you forget that it is set on!

The LAYER command is used to make a new layer called 'floor' which is then used for the outline of the building. Later additions to the drawing can be put on other layers. The OFFSET command is a convenient method of duplicating lines to show the double skin of the wall because the command remains active. The COPY command gives a similar effect, as shown for the internal walls.

The openings in the walls are made with multiple uses of the BREAK command. The edges of the openings are closed with the LINE command, helped by a ZOOM view and use of the object snap target box. The OSNAP command is used to set object snap into 'running mode' which produces the target box whenever you pick a point in any future command. Object snap can also be temporarily summoned in 'override mode' when picking any point; by picking the asterisks at the top of the menu, for example.

The SAVE command is used to store the drawing as a file on the computer disk. If necessary, a filename must be preceded by the drive letter or the subdirectory where it is to be stored. For example: *B:cabin1* for storage on floppy disk B; or *work\cabin1* for storage in a subdirectory called work. The SAVE command should be used regularly during a drawing session, not just at the end.

An AutoCAD drawing can be printed out on many sizes of paper in different drawing scales. The sequence used here assumes that you are making a quick draft on A4 paper in a dot-matrix or laser printer. In this example we assume that 1 drawing unit on screen equals 1 metre in reality. At printout we choose a scale that 20 mm on paper equals 1 drawing unit (1 metre). This scale is the same as an architectural scale of 1:50 (because 20 mm equals 1000 mm) and fits onto A4 paper.

If you are a little confused by this topic of scales on screen and on paper, then you are not alone. It is often easier to experiment on your plotter or printer than to read (or write) about it. You can check the scale of a final drawing by using a ruler. Keep a note of your settings.

The instructions

Follow the sequences of instructions listed under the 'Activity' columns and remember the following points:

- Commands can be 'selected' from menus or by typing command words.
- The layout of menus varies with your version of AutoCAD.
- Points can be 'picked' by pointing on screen and clicking, or by typing in coordinates.
- The prompt line at the bottom of the screen shows the current options.
- Use the **HELP** command or **?** for on-screen information.
- Use **Ctrl-C** to cancel a wrong sequence and start again.
- The **U** for Undo command is useful for some mistakes.
- Boxes in the margin refer to a group of prompt pages in Part One of the book where commands are explained and illustrated.

Activity	Comment
Select 1	from Main Menu.
Enter *cabin1=wksh1*	to start new drawing file with same settings as standard worksheet.
Set **ORTHO** to ON	to keep all lines at right angles. Use function key F7 on PCs.
Select **LAYER** command or use pulldown menu	to modify layer settings.
Choose **Make** option	to create new layer and make it current.
Enter *Floor*	as name of new layer.
Choose **Thaw** option	to unfreeze the border layer.
Enter *Border*	as name of layer to thaw.
[RETURN]	to complete command.
Select **LINE** command	to draw outline of building
Pick 2, 3	as start point of line.
Pick 2, 7	as second point.
Pick 10, 7	as third point.
Pick 10, 3	as fourth point.
Choose **Close** option	to complete building outline.
Select **OFFSET** command	
Enter 0.2	as offset distance.
Pick any point on top wall	as object to offset.
Pick any point inside shell	as side to offset. Offset command remains active.
Repeat offset procedure for other 3 walls.	All walls should be doubled.
[RETURN]	to complete command.
Select **SNAP** command	to change snap setting.

See also
UTILITIES
Prompt pages

Layer FLOOR Ortho Snap   0.000,0.000

Shell of building before use of FILLET command to clean overlaps at /corners.

Activity	Comment
Enter 0.2	as new SNAP setting.
Select **FILLET** command	to fix overlapping corner lines.
Pick 9, 6.8 or similar	as first object.
Pick 9.8, 6 or similar	as second object.
[RETURN]	to repeat FILLET command.
Repeat fillet procedure for other 3 corners.	All corners should be joined without overlap.
Select **LINE** command	to draw internal walls.
Pick 7, 6.8	as start point of line.
Pick 7, 3.2	as end point of line.
[RETURN]	to end line.
[RETURN]	to repeat LINE command.
Pick 7, 5	as start point of line.
Pick 9.8, 5	as end point of line.
[RETURN]	to end line.

See also
CHANGES
Prompt pages

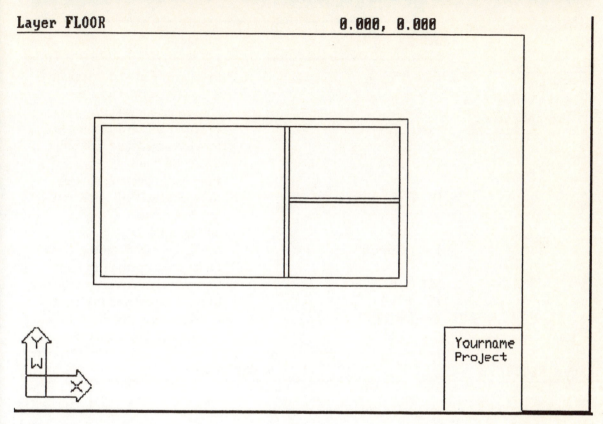

Layer FLOOR   0.000, 0.000

Walls and partitions.

Activity	Comment
Select **COPY** command	to double internal walls.
Pick 8, 5 or any point on line	to select object. Or use Last option.
[RETURN]	to complete selection.
Pick 8, 5 or any point on line	as base point.
Enter @0, 0.1	as relative x,y displacement of 100 mm upwards.
[RETURN]	to repeat COPY command.
Pick 7, 6 or any point on line	to select object.
[RETURN]	to complete selection.
Pick 7, 6 or any point on line	as base point.
Enter @–0.1, 0	as relative displacement of 100 mm leftwards.
Select **REDRAW** command	to clear screen marks.
Select **BREAK** command	to make openings in outer walls.

Activity	Comment
Pick 3, 3	to select object and first point.
Pick 6, 3	as second point. Outer patio opening appears.
[RETURN]	to repeat BREAK command.
Pick 3, 3.2	to select object and first point.
Pick 6, 3.2	as second point. Inner patio opening appears.
[RETURN]	to repeat BREAK command.
Pick 8, 3	to select object and first point.
Enter @0.8, 0	as relative x, y distances. Outer door opening appears.
[RETURN]	to repeat BREAK command.
Pick 8, 3.2	to select object and first point.
Enter @0.8, 0	as relative x, y distances. Inner door opening appears.

See also
CHANGES
Prompt pages

Layer FLOOR   0.000,0.000

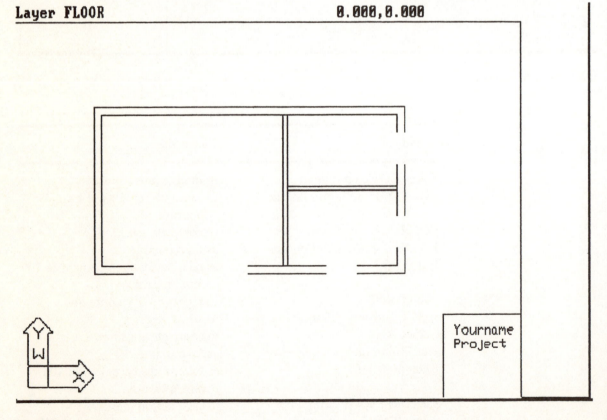

External openings.

Activity	Comment
[RETURN]	to repeat BREAK command.
Pick 10, 6.4	to select object and first point.
Pick 10, 5.6	as second point. Outer window opening appears.
[RETURN]	to repeat BREAK command.
Pick 9.8, 6.4	to select object and first point.
Pick 9.8, 5.6	as second point. Inner window opening appears.
[RETURN]	to repeat BREAK command.
Pick 10, 4.4	to select object and first point.
Pick 10, 3.6	as second point. Outer window opening appears.
[RETURN]	to repeat BREAK command.
Pick 9.8, 4.4	to select object and first point.
Pick 9.8, 3.6	as second point. Inner window opening appears.

See also
OUTPUTS
Prompt pages

Activity	Comment
Use **REDRAW** command	to remove screen marks.
Select **ZOOM** command	to enlarge area at right.
Choose **Window** option	
Pick 6, 7 or near	as first corner of window.
Pick 11, 2 or near	as second corner of window.
Select **BREAK** command	to make openings in internal walls.
Pick 7, 4	to select object and first point.
Enter @0, 0.8	as relative x, y distance. Door opening appears.
[RETURN]	to repeat BREAK command.
Pick 7, 6	to select object and first point.
Enter @0, –0.8	as relative x, y distance. Door opening appears.

See also
UTILITIES
Prompt pages

Activity	Comment
Set **SNAP** to OFF	use function key F9 on PCs.
[RETURN]	to repeat BREAK command.
Enter 6.9, 4	to select object and first point.
Enter @0, 0.8	as relative x, y distance. Door opening appears.
[RETURN]	to repeat BREAK command.
Enter 6.9, 6	to select object and first point.
Enter @0, –0.8	as relative x, y distance.
Select **OSNAP** command	To set running mode.
Choose **ENDpoint**	as OSNAP mode.
Select **LINE** command	to close edges of doors and windows.

Layer FLOOR   9.185, 3.725

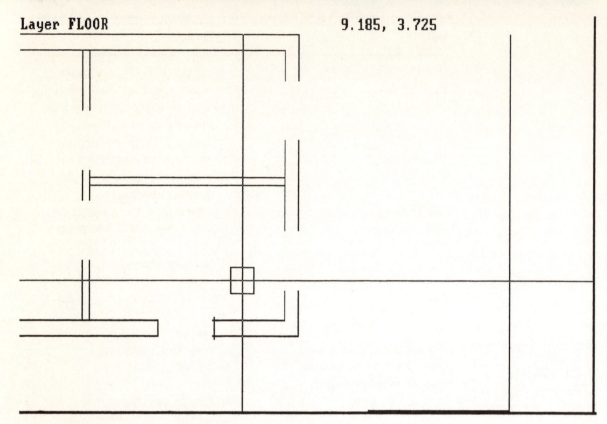

Use of OSNAP target to locate edges at openings.

Activity	Comment
Pick 8, 3	with help of OSNAP target.
Pick 8, 3.2	with help of OSNAP target.
[RETURN]	to complete LINE command. Edge of door reveal is drawn.
[RETURN]	to repeat LINE command.
Repeat above LINE procedure to close edges of all visible doors and windows.	
Select **OSNAP** command	to cancel running mode.
[RETURN]	to cancel current mode.
Select **PAN** command	to bring left of drawing into view.
Pick 7, 3 or near	as Pan displacement.
Pick 12, 3	as second point. Screen view moves over drawing.

See also
OUTPUTS
Prompt pages

Activity	Comment
Use **LINE** command	to close edges of patio door. Select OSNAP override (****) to help.
Select **ZOOM** command	
Choose **All** option	to restore full view.
Select **SAVE** command	
Enter *cabin1*	as filename to store drawing. Add pathname if required.
Select **PRPLOT** (PRINTER PLOT)	to make draft printout on fast printer.
Choose *Limits* option	as part of drawing to plot.
Enter *Yes*	to question about making changes to settings.
Repeat [RETURN]	to accept most of the settings as standard.

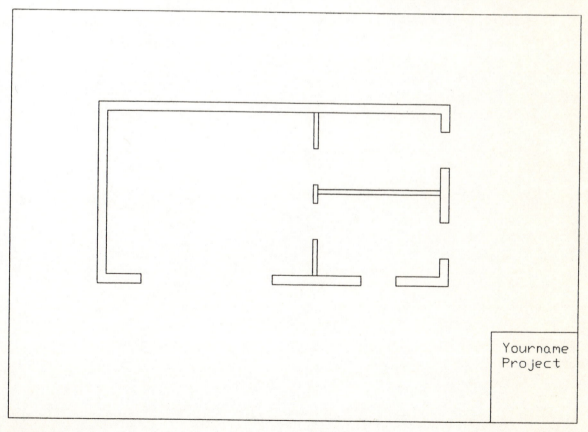

Final drawing.

Activity	Comment
Enter *Yes*	to rotate plot 90 degrees.
Enter *20=1*	to specify scale of 20 mm = 1 drawing unit (same as 1:50).
Follow screen instructions to start printing	Check that proposed plotting area suits your printer.
Select **QUIT** command	to leave drawing.
Enter *Y*	to agree to abandon drawing and return to Main Menu.

Components

This section adds windows, doors and furniture to the simple *cabin* building and demonstrates how any 'part' of a drawing can be used many times. Once a component has been stored it can be imported and used in the current drawing or in any other drawing. During the insertion of components into a drawing you are given control over their position, size and layout.

A system of component 'libraries' are an important method for CAD efficiency. You should aim to build up sets of useful components and give them filenames which make sense to yourself and to others. Libraries of standard parts used in various industries are also available from outside sources, such as the RIBACAD components shown at the end of the section.

AutoCAD commands and features used in this section include the following:

- LAYER
- FILL
- PLINE
- LINE
- BLOCK
- WBLOCK

- INSERT
- OSNAP
- ZOOM
- ARC
- OOPS
- END

The techniques

The first sequence of instructions makes a new drawing file called *cabin2* which is based on the previously saved drawing called *cabin1*. The LAYER command prepares a new layer for the windows.

The PLINE and LINE command are used to draw the window component in the middle of the screen. The BLOCK command then stores the component into the current drawing file. Even if you don't use the component in the drawing, its details are stored in the drawing file on disk.

The WBLOCK command stores the window component as an external drawing file which can later be called into any drawing. Any other part of the drawing can also be selected and saved externally.

The INSERT command is used to recall the window block and place it into the three window openings, changing the size and rotation of the window to suit each opening. The convenience of this technique is one reason why we draw separate window lines rather than share lines with the walls.

The door is drawn in its position with the LINE and ARC commands and it is then stored with the BLOCK command. The OOPS command is used to immediately insert the door block. The ZOOM command is used as appropriate so that each area of the drawing is large enough for the object snap mode to find the MIDpoint of lines.

Instructions

Follow the sequences of instructions listed under the 'Activity' columns and remember the following points:

- Commands can be 'selected' from menus or by typing command words.
- Points can be 'picked' by pointing on screen and clicking or by typing in coordinates.
- The prompt line at the bottom of the screen gives the next options.
- Use **Ctrl-C** to cancel a wrong sequence and start again.
- The U for Undo command is useful for mistakes.
- Boxes in the margin refer to a group of prompt pages in Part one of the book where commands are explained and illustrated.

Activity	Comment
Select 1	to open drawing from Main Menu.
Enter *cabin2=cabin1*	to open new drawing based on existing building shell.
Select **Layer** command	to start new layer.
Choose **Make** option	to choose new layer and make it current.
Enter *Window*	as name of new layer.
[RETURN]	to complete command.
Select **FILL** command	
Choose **OFF** option	to produce empty polylines.
Check **SNAP** is ON	use function key F9 on PCs.
Select **PLINE** command	to draw window outline in any blank area of screen.
Pick 4, 5	as first point.

See also
UTILITIES
Prompt pages

Layer WINDOW   0.000,0.000

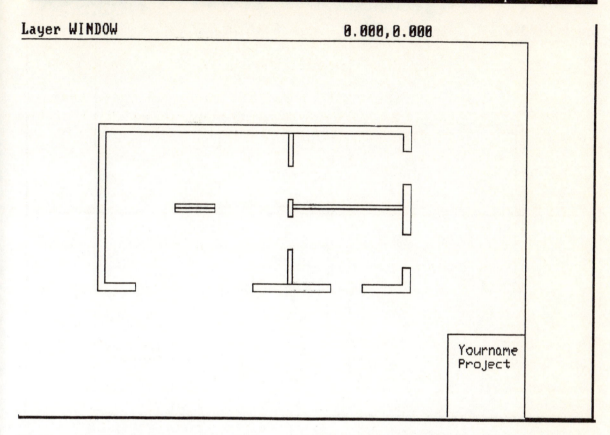

Yourname
Project

Window created in temporary position before storage by BLOCK command.

Activity	Comment
Choose **Width** option	
Enter 0.2	as starting width.
[RETURN]	to keep ending width as 0.2.
Pick 5, 5	as second point.
[RETURN]	to complete command.
Select **LINE** command	to draw line inside window.
Pick 4, 5	as first point. Pick 5,5 as second point.
[RETURN]	to complete command.
Set **SNAP** to OFF	use function key F9 on PCs.
Select **BLOCK** command	to store window as part.
Enter *window1*	as block name.
Enter 4, 5	as insertion base point.
Pick all parts of window drawing	as objects to select.

See also
ENTITIES
Prompt pages

Layer WINDOW   6.443,4.817

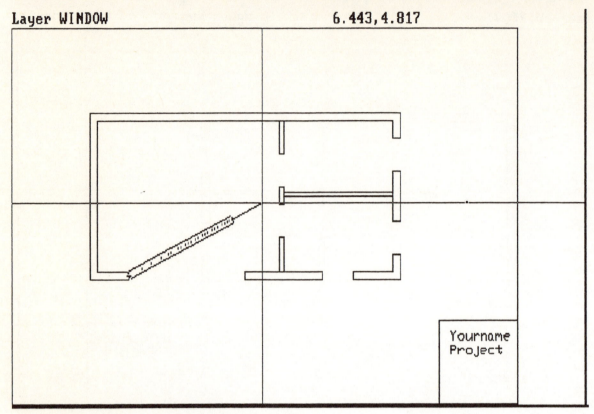

Long window being positioned by INSERT command.

Activity	Comment
[RETURN]	when selection is complete.
	Window disappears but is stored as part within drawing file.
Use **WBLOCK** command	to store window drawing as separate drawing file.
Enter *window1*	as filename, with pathname if required.
Enter *window1*	as block to store.
Select **INSERT** command	to insert long front window.
Enter *window1*	as block name.
Pick 3, 3.1	as insertion point in middle end of wall.
Enter 3	as X scale factor.
Enter 1	as Y scale factor.
[RETURN]	to accept rotation angle of 0.
	Window drawing is now placed into wall opening.

Activity	Comment
Use **ZOOM** command	to enlarge view of right side of building.
Select **INSERT** command	to insert window into right-hand wall.
Enter *window1*	as block name.
Pick 9.9, 6.4	as insertion point – use OSNAP to help select point.
Enter 0.8	as X scale.
Enter 1	as Y scale.
Enter –90	as rotation angle.
	Window drawing is placed into opening.
Repeat **INSERT** procedure	for other window opening in right hand wall.

See also
OUTPUTS
Prompt pages

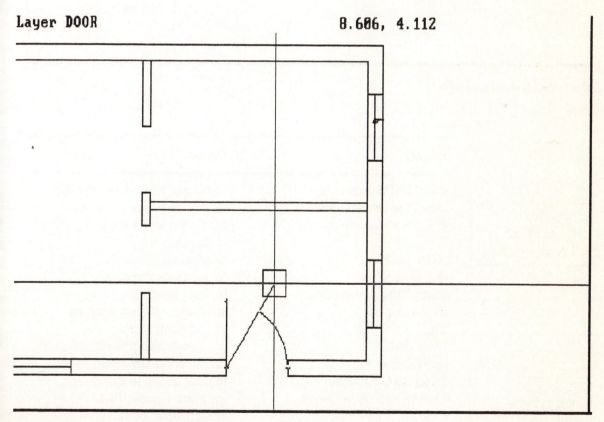

Layer DOOR   8.606, 4.112

Construction of door with aid of OSNAP.

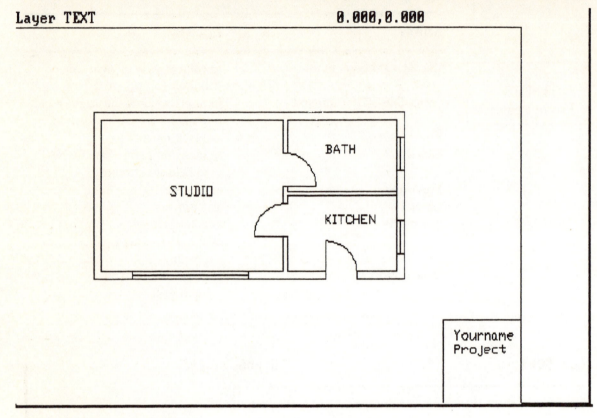

Layer TEXT   0.000,0.000

STUDIO

BATH

KITCHEN

Yourname
Project

Labels added onto TEXT layer.

	Activity	Comment
	Use **ZOOM** command	to enlarge front door opening.
	Select **Layer** command	to start new layer.
See also **UTILITIES** Prompt pages	Choose **Make** option	to choose new layer and make it current.
	Enter *Door*	as name of new layer.
	[RETURN]	to complete command.
	Select **LINE** command	to draw door.
	Pick 8, 3.1	at left side of door opening.
	Enter @0.8<90	as end point of open door.
	[RETURN]	to complete command.
	Set **SNAP** to OFF	use function key F9 on PCs.
See also **ENTITIES** Prompt pages	Select **ARC** command	to draw swing line of door.
	Choose **S, C, E** option	for Start, Centre, End.
	Pick 8.8, 3.1	as start point of arc.
	Pick 8, 3.1	as centre point of arc.

Activity	Comment
Activate **OSNAP**	to snap onto points.
Choose OSNAP **END** option	to pick following point.
Pick swing end of door	as end point of arc.
Use **BLOCK** command	to store door drawing as part within drawing.
Enter *door1*	as block name.
Enter 8, 3.1	as insertion base point.
Pick all parts of door	as objects to select.
[RETURN]	to complete selection. Door disappears but is stored as part within drawing file.
Use **OOPS** command	to restore door in current drawing on screen.
Use **WBLOCK** command	to store door drawing as separate drawing file.

See also
ENTITIES
Prompt pages

Layer FURNITUR   6.000,4.000

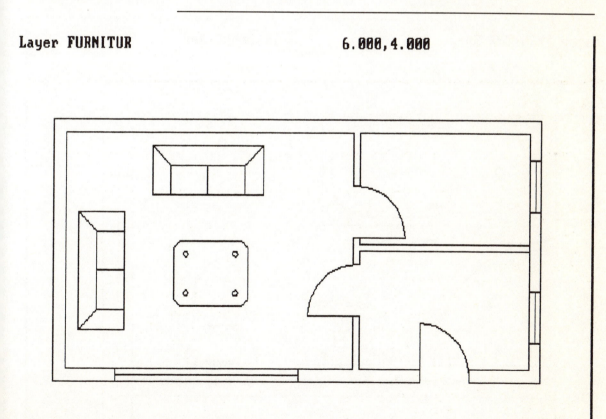

Insertion of furniture from previous drawings.

Activity	Comment
Enter *door1*	as filename, with pathname if required.
Enter *door1*	as block to store.
Repeat **INSERT** procedure	for internal doors.
Use **COPY, MIRROR, MOVE** commands	to help position doors.
Select **ZOOM** command	
Choose **All** option	to restore original view.
Choose **END** command	to save file and return to Main menu.

Further activities

Use the DTEXT command to write the labels such as 'BATH' and 'KITCHEN' as shown on the drawing. Use a separate layer such as the

Layer FURNITUR Snap   10.200,7.200

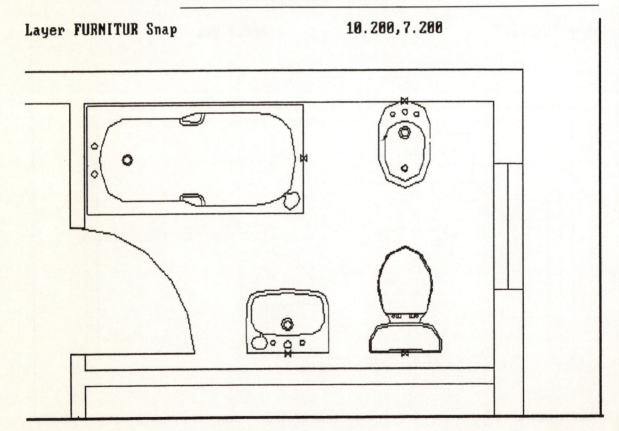

Insertion of sanitary ware from RIBACAD library.

'text' layer which already exists in the standard worksheet used for this drawing.

Use the BREAK command to clean up the junctions between the walls. Use the object snap aid to pick the correct intersections.

Change the long front window to a patio door. Erase the existing window, change to the 'door' layer, and draw the door. Even if you choose to make the door look similar to the window there will be advantages in having separate layers, especially for items at different levels.

Use the INSERT command to import some external items. If AutoCAD finds that a named part doesn't exist as a block within the current drawing then it looks for an outside drawing with that name. The example has used the *table* and *sofa* drawings of the previous exercise.

The 'scale factor' options of the INSERT command allow you to adjust for the discrepancies in size between the drawings. Try using factors of 0.1 and 0.2 in this case. The ROTATE and MOVE commands can be used for final positioning of the furniture.

The bathroom example shows insertions of Ideal-Standard Limited sanitary ware imported from the RIBACAD library of construction components. Such component drawings, available without charge from RIBA Services Ltd, also contain well-organised layers giving textual information and different drawings of the object suitable for different scales. Imported layers will automatically be created in your host drawing and can be frozen or thawed to suit your needs.

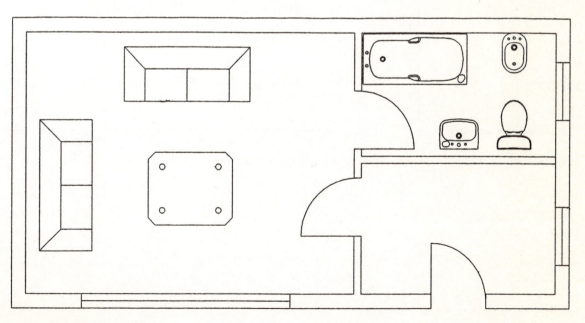

Completed drawing.

F24/
Claybricks to BS 3921

50 mm cavity with 25 mm
insulation batt

115 mm Thermalite Turbo blocks

13 mm Lightweight Plaster

Compressive strength 2.8N/mm^2

U Value: 0.44 W/m^2 deg C

Standard details and optional connotations from RIBACAD library of components.

3D Views

Whether they are an attraction or distraction, three-dimensional views exert a strong appeal. As shown in a previous section, AutoCAD can transform a 2D drawing into 3D with just a few commands; provided that you have entered enough information about the third dimension. You can continue to draw while in 3D and continue to use most AutoCAD commands.

Although CAD systems can create 'pop-up' pictures from 2D drawings, it is a good idea to keep the idea of a 'visualisation' separate from the idea of 'true' solids. AutoCAD initially shows a 'wire-frame' view of an object which can be made to appear more solid by hiding those lines which could not be seen from the chosen viewpoint. To improve the visualisation effects, AutoCAD can change the parallel lines of the initial 3D view to the converging lines of a perspective view.

AutoCAD commands and features used in this section include the following:

- 3DFACE
- ZOOM
- CHANGE
- REGEN
- VPOINT
- REDRAW
- DVIEW
- CHANGE
- VPORTS
- OSNAP
- HIDE
- SCALE

The techniques

The first sequence of activities opens a completely new drawing file called *cabroof* based on the standard prototype or worksheet drawing previously created and saved as *wksh1*. The aim is to draw a simple roof shape, sloping in one direction, which can be viewed in 3D and then added to the drawing of the cabin, or any other rectangular building.

The use of the 3DFACE command to draw the roof surfaces initially gives the same effect as drawing with simple lines but the 3DFACE command gives a solid or opaque look to surfaces when the HIDE command is given later. Outlines made with simple lines can only be extruded upwards.

The flat surface of the horizontal ceiling and the sloping roof are drawn with the 3DFACE command. You can enter the z-coordinates for those points on the high end of the roof. All the other points, at ceiling level, are assumed to have the same height as the current construction plane (elevation), which is zero.

The VPOINT command generates a 3D wireframe view of the surfaces drawn so far. The 3D view is kept on screen and used while drawing the vertical faces on the three sides of the roof shape. The grid snap and the object snap aids are both used to identify the points accurately.

3D Cabin

The second drawing sequence, titled *3D cabin* develops the previously created outline of a building saved in a file called *cabin1*. You can use any similar drawing although, to keep the visualisation process effective, it is easiest to operate only on the walls.

The CHANGE command is used to give the walls a suitable extruded height (termed 'thickness') and a new layer is created for the roof. The roof shape created in the first sequence is imported into the drawing. The INSERT command looks first for a block saved within the current drawing and if there is no block with the appropriate name, as in this case, then any drawing file with that name is inserted just like a block.

The CHANGE command is also used to alter the construction plane (elevation) of the bottom of the roof to match the top of the walls. The area of the roof is enlarged with the SCALE command in order to give an overhang.

A VPOINT command creates an initial 3D view and the VPORTS command is used to split the screen into three 'viewports'. The VPOINT and HIDE commands are used to set different views for the split screens.

The DVIEW command creates a perspective type of 3D view with vanishing-point perspective. There are several methods of setting this type of view and you should experiment with using the sliding indicator bars. Remember that these settings of camera, target and distance are relative to the previous setting.

Setting the distance option of the DVIEW command also turns on the perspective mode which remains in effect until the *off* option is used. For a distinct perspective effect the target position should be some distance away from the the camera position.

Instructions

Follow the sequences of instructions listed under the 'Activity' columns and remember the following points:

- Commands can be 'selected' from menus or by typing command words.
- Points can be 'picked' by pointing on screen and clicking or by typing in coordinates.
- The prompt line at the bottom of the screen gives the next options.
- Use **Ctrl-C** to cancel a wrong sequence and start again.
- The **U** for Undo command is useful for mistakes.
- Boxes in the margin refer to a group of prompt pages in Part One of the book where commands are explained and illustrated.

3D Roof

Activity	Comment
Select 1	from Main Menu.
type *cabroof=wksh1*	as filename for roof drawing.
Set **GRID** to ON	use function key F7 on PCs.
Set **SNAP** to ON	use function key F9 on PCs.
Set **COORDS** to ON	use function key F6 on PCs.
Select **3DFACE** command	to draw ceiling surface.
Pick 2, 3	as first point.
Pick 10, 3	as second point.
Pick 10, 7	as third point.
Pick 2, 7	as fourth point.
[RETURN]	to complete command.
Select **3DFACE** command	to draw sloping roof surface.
Pick 2, 3	as first point.
Pick 10, 3	as second point.
Pick 10, 7,1	as third point, with Z height.
Pick 2, 7,1	as fourth point, with Z height.
[RETURN]	to complete command.
Select **VPOINT** command	as start 3D view.
Enter 1, –1, 1	as viewpoint coordinates.
	Or use screen viewpoint systems.
	Roof and ceiling surfaces appear hinged at one edge.
Select **3DFACE**	to fill in sides of roof in 3D mode.
Pick 10, 3	as first point.
Pick 10, 7	as second point.
Set **SNAP** to OFF	
Activate **OSNAP**	
Choose **INTersection** option	from OSNAP menu.

See also
ENTITIES
Prompt pages

See also
OUTPUTS
Prompt pages

Layer 0 Snap   6.000, 14.000

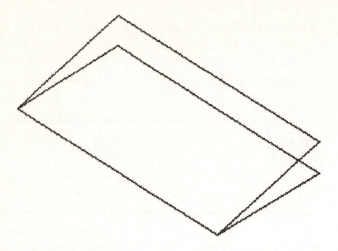

VPOINT display of ceiling and roof surfaces.

Activity	Comment
Pick any point on roof line near top right	as third point.
[RETURN]	
[RETURN]	to complete command.
Repeat last **3DFACE** procedure	to fill in other side of roof.
Repeat last **3DFACE** procedure	to fill in rear edge of roof.
Set **GRID** command to OFF	use function key F7 on PCs.
Select **HIDE** command	to remove hidden lines.
Choose **Yes** option	to confirm, if necessary.
Repeat **VPOINT** and **HIDE** command to see visualisation from other viewpoints	Check views from other sides and from beneath.
Use **ZOOM** command as necessary	choose **All** option.
Use **REGEN** command as necessary	to restore damaged lines.

See also
OUTPUTS
Prompt pages

Layer 0   6.000, 12.000

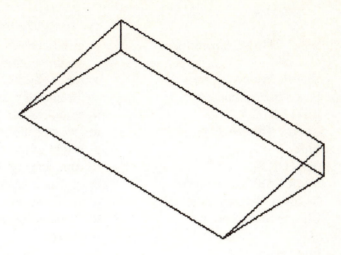

Completion of side surfaces by 3DFACE command.

Activity	Comment
Select **VPOINT** command	to restore plan view.
Enter 0, 0,1	or choose **Plan** option.
Select **ZOOM** command	
Choose **All** option	to restore full drawing.
Select **END** command	to save current drawing under filename *cabroof*.

3D Cabin

Activity	Comment
Select 1	from Main Menu.
Enter *cabin-3d=cabin1*	to start new drawing file based on existing building shell.

Activity	Comment
Check that FLOOR layer is current	Shown at top of screen.
	Or use default '0' layer.
Select **CHANGE** command	to give thickness (height) to building outline.
Choose **Window** option	to select objects.
Pick Window corners	to include all parts of building.
[ENTER]	to complete selection.
Choose **Thickness** option	to give extruded thickness.
Enter 2.5	as height of building.
[RETURN]	to complete command.
Select **LAYER** command	to start new layer.
Or use pull-down menu	to modify layer.
Choose **Make** option	to create new layer and make it current.
Enter *roof*	as name of new layer.
[RETURN]	to complete command.
Choose **INSERT** command	to import a stored drawing.
Enter *cabroof*	as name of roof drawing file.
Pick 0, 0	as insertion point.
Enter 1	as X scale factor.
[RETURN]	to accept same Y scale factor.
[RETURN]	to accept rotation of 0.
Select **CHANGE** command	to change base level of roof.
Pick any point on roof outline	but avoid picking floor. Check that roof (only) appears dotted.
[RETURN]	to complete selection.
Choose **Elev** option	to change base height.
Enter 2.5	as start of roof level.
[RETURN]	to complete command.
Select **SCALE** command	to enlarge area of roof and overhang walls.
Choose **Last** option	to select objects.
[RETURN]	to complete selection.
Pick 6, 5 at centre of roof	as base point.
Enter 1.1	as scale factor.
Select **REDRAW** command	to restore full drawing.
Select **VPOINT** command	to start 3D view.
[RETURN]	
Enter –1, –1, 0.5	as viewpoint coordinates, or use screen viewpoint systems.
Select **VPOINT** command	to restore plan view.

See also
CHANGES
Prompt pages

See also
ENTITIES
Prompt pages

See also
CHANGES
Prompt pages

See also
OUTPUTS
Prompt pages

Layer ROOF   4.219,3.011

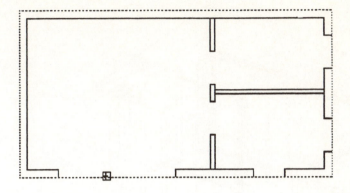

Roof inserted and selected for CHANGE command.

Activity	Comment
Enter 0, 0, 1	or choose Plan option.
Select **VPORTS**	to set number of screen viewports.
Choose **3** option	to divide screen into 3 viewports.
[RETURN]	
Move cursor to top viewport	to choose new viewport.
Pick any point	to activate new viewport.
Select **VPOINT** command	to restore plane view.
Enter 0, 0, 1	or choose Plan option.
	Display changes in top viewport.
Move cursor to large viewport	to choose new viewport.
Pick any point	to activate new viewport.
Select **ZOOM** command	to fill large viewport.
Use **PAN** command	to centre drawing in large viewport.
Select **HIDE** command	to remove hidden lines.

Layer ROOF   18.851,6.296

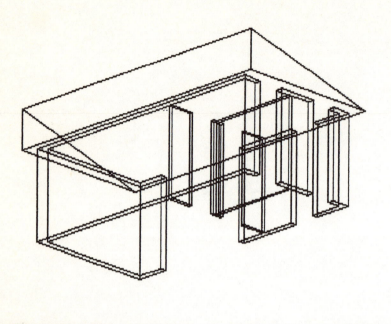

Wireframe effect of VPOINT command.

Activity	Comment
Choose **Yes** option	to confirm, if necessary.
Select **VPORTS** command	to reset screen divisions.
Choose **Single** option	to restore single screen.
Select **SAVE** command	to save current drawing under filename *cabroof*.
Use **LAYER** command to freeze *Roof* layer	or use pull-down menu.
Select **VPOINT** command [RETURN]	to see parallel 3D view.
Enter 3, –3, 2	as viewpoint coordinates or or use screen viewpoint system.
Select **DVIEW** command [RETURN]	to see perspective 3D view.
	in response to select objects.
	'House' icon appears on screen as guide to effect of view changes.

See also
OUTPUTS
Prompt pages

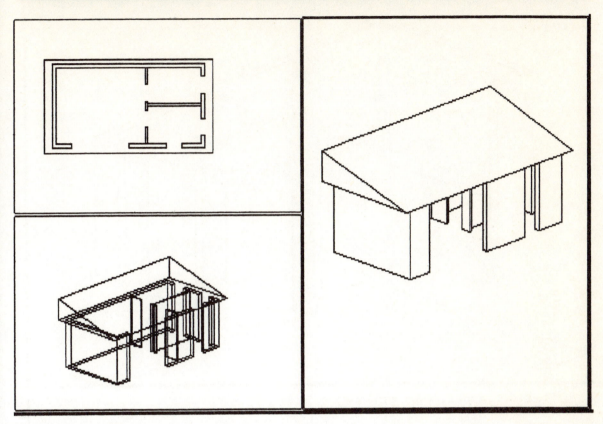

Effect of VPORTS command.

Activity	Comment
Choose **Points** option	
Enter 6, 5, 1	as target point.
Enter 20, –8, 8	as camera point.
Choose **Distance** option	to turn on perspective mode.
Enter 16	
Repeat **DVIEW** command	
Use slider bars	to see different perspective views.
Use **OFF** option	to turn perspective off.
Select **QUIT** command	to leave drawing without saving recent changes.
Enter *Y*	to confirm quit action and return to Main Menu.

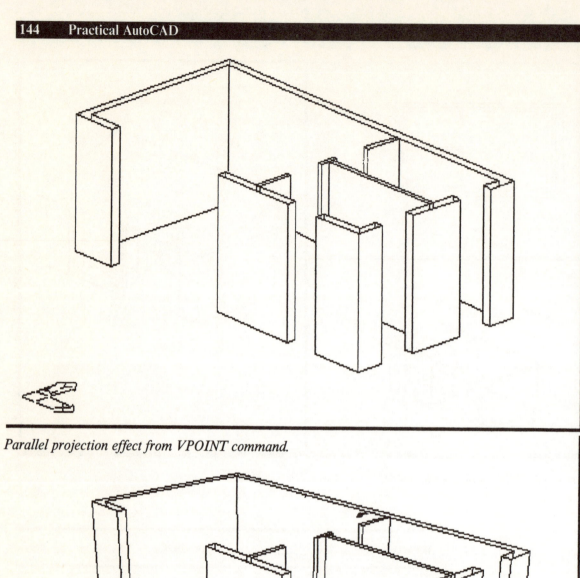

Parallel projection effect from VPOINT command.

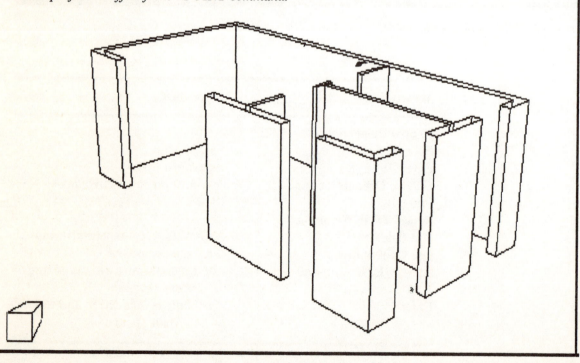

Vanishing point or perspective effect from DVIEW command.

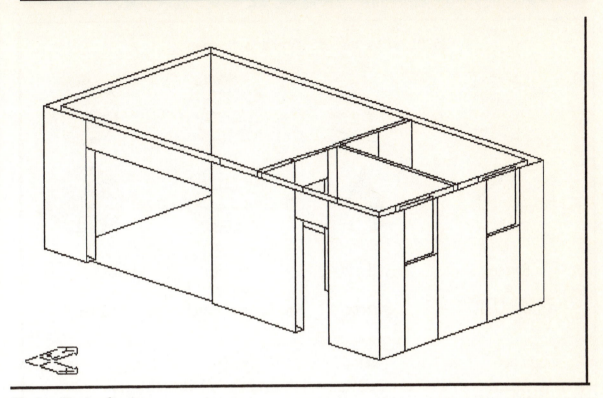

Further 3D visualisation.

Further activities

More elaborate 3D visualisations of a buildings can be developed from a drawing such as *cabin2*. The appropriate construction plane (elevation) and thickness of every component must be specified. The CHANGE command can be used to change existing objects. The UCS command and SETVAR (THICKNESS) can make settings for future objects.

Similar types of component, such as windows, should be grouped in their own layers. Make new layers as appropriate and, if necessary, use the CHANGE command to move components to a new layer. When it is difficult to distinguish separate layers or to select objects, then use the Freeze option of the LAYER command.

AutoCAD has additional commands – RULESURF, TABSURF, REVSURF and EDGESURF – which can simplify the creation of a variety of 3D surfaces.

3D Objects and 3D Surface Commands

☐ ☐ ☐ ☐

☐ ☐ ☐ ☐

Surface
of
☐ REVOLUTION   ☐ RULED
Surface   ☐ EDGE
Defined
Surface Patch   ☐ TABULATED
Surface

Set
☐ SURFTAB1   Set
☐ SURFTAB2   ☐   ☐ Exit

Screen menu for 3D drawing.

Developments

Previous exercises have shown that AutoCAD often offers several methods of creating the same-looking drawing on screen and paper. If the drawing file is used just for a single view then it possibly doesn't matter how the objects were constructed. But if the drawing file is to be 'developed' and used for many purposes, then the hidden features of the objects will keep affecting future use.

For example, single entities, such as lines, behave differently to grouped entities, such as those in polylines and blocks. We have seen how the nature of the entity is even more important for 3D solids and visualisation. The organisation of layers, colours and linetypes is also vital in the control of large drawings and this exercise gives a glimpse of the necessity for individuals and offices to standardise on methods of working.

AutoCAD commands and features used in this section include the following:

- LIMITS
- INSERT
- EXPLODE
- ZOOM
- AREA
- MIRROR
- MOVE
- FILLET
- BLOCK
- LINETYPE
- LTSCALE
- LIST
- DBLIST

The techniques

The example shown here uses a drawing from previous exercise but you could use any of your drawings. The instructions, given in outline form, can also be read for ideas rather than used as a strict exercise.

The drawing of the cabin imported into this site drawing is one of the simpler versions, before more internal details such as furniture were added. In practice you can use the same drawing file for both large scale and detail work by keeping information on layers which can be frozen when they are not appropriate. For example, different sizes of paper need different scales of text and these can be kept on separate layers.

AutoCAD has a number of 'inquiry' command whose results are

displayed here. The ID command reveals the coordinates of any point, which is especially useful for revealing the value of the third-dimensional z-coordinate when it is not apparent on the drawing. The AREA command calculates the area and perimeter contained within specified points.

Numerical descriptions of points and distances – parametric details – are given by the LIST and DBLIST commands. The LIST command describes chosen objects while DBLIST describes all objects and other details of the drawing.

Instructions

The instructions under the 'Activity' columns are an outline of the methods used to develop the drawing. Details of the commands have been given in previous exercises.

- Commands can be 'selected' from menus or by typing command words.
- Points can be 'picked' by pointing on screen and clicking or by typing in coordinates.
- The prompt line at the bottom of the screen gives the next options.
- Use **Ctrl-C** to cancel a wrong sequence and start again.
- The **U** for Undo command is useful for mistakes.
- Boxes in the margin refer to a group of prompt pages in Part One of the book where commands are explained and illustrated.

Outline instructions

Activity	Comment
Start a new drawing to contain a complete building site.	
Use **LIMITS** command to set a size such as 29 by 20 metres.	Or try the menu SETUP option which is an AutoLisp routine.
Use **UNITS** command to set decimal-type units.	
Use **GRID** command to set at 1	
Use **SNAP** command to set at 0.5.	Or appropriate values.
Set **SNAP** and **GRID** to ON	as appropriate during drawing.
Create and set a new layer called 'Building'	The 'layers' dialogue box from the pull-down menu is useful.
Use **INSERT** command to import *cabin2* drawing.	Or use any building drawing.

See also
UTILITIES
Prompt pages

See also
ENTITIES
Prompt pages

Activity	Comment
Use 0, 0 as insertion point and choose appropriate scale.	
Suppress 'border' layer if border is visible around cabin.	
Use **EXPLODE** command to disassemble imported block.	Pick any point on cabin.
	No change is seen but future behaviour is affected.
Use **ZOOM** command to magnify area near cabin.	Use ZOOM and PAN as needed.
Use **AREA** command on cabin	Pick 4 points on the perimeter.
Use **MIRROR** command to produce two cabins, back to back.	Pick rear wall as mirror line.
Use **MOVE** command to adjust width of party wall between cabins.	

Layer BUILDING Snap   −1.00,2.00

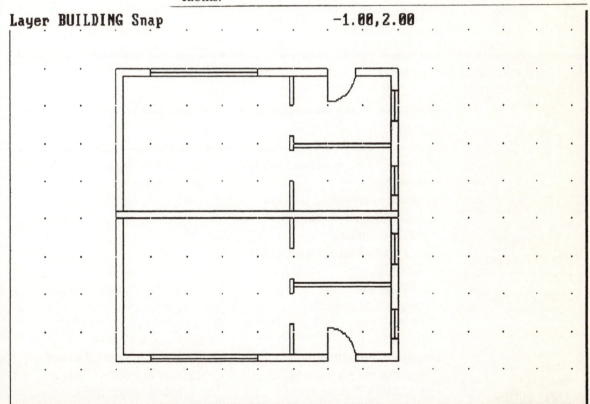

Double building constructed using MIRROR command.

Layer ROAD Snap   0.00, 0.00

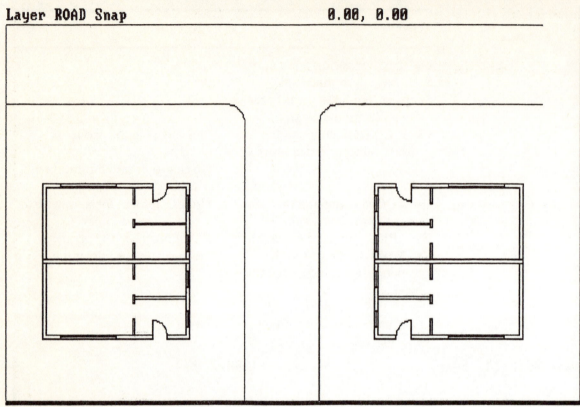

Road layout added on separate layer.

	Activity	Comment
	Create and set a new layer called 'Road'	The layers' dialogue box from the pull-down menu is useful.
	Draw the road layout	
See also **CHANGES** Prompt pages	Use the **FILLET** command to produce curves	Set fillet radius to, say, 1 m.
	Create and set a new layer called 'Drain'.	
	Use **SNAP** command to adjust snap setting to 0.25	or other appropriate settings.
	Draw single examples of drainage symbols.	Such as inspection chamber, gully, and soil pipe.
	Use **BLOCK** command to store symbols within drawing.	WBLOCK can be used to store symbols in external files.
See also **UTILITIES** Prompt pages	Use **LINETYPE** command to set new style of line such as 'hidden' or 'dashed'.	Use ? option to see styles.

Layer DRAIN   1.00,2.00

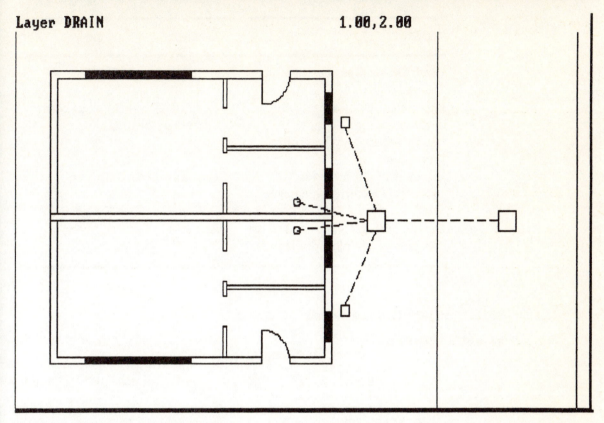

Drainage details added to one building.

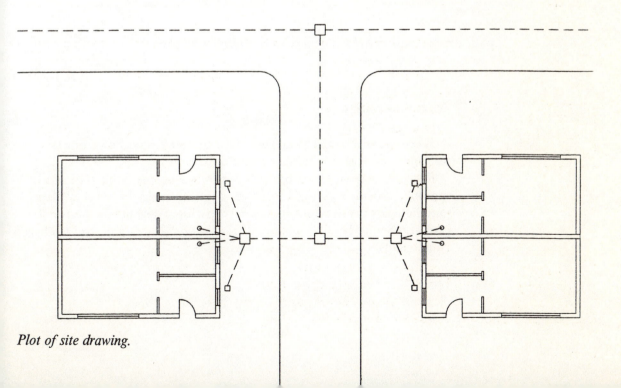

Plot of site drawing.

Activity	Comment
Use **LTSCALE** so set size of line units, such as 1.	
Experiment with the AREA command.	Use OSNAP to help select corner points of the area.
Use Ctrl-Q to turn the printer echo on.	
Use the **LIST** command.	Select any object on screen.
Use **Ctrl-Q** to turn printer echo off.	
Use the **DBLIST** command to see details of complete drawing.	Use Ctrl-C to cancel if necessary.

```
   LIST
Select objects: 1 selected, 1 found.

Select objects:
                BLOCK REFERENCE  Layer: DRAIN
                GULLEY
           at point, X=     10.25  Y=       4.50  Z=       0.00
             X scale factor    1.0000
             Y scale factor    1.0000
        rotation angle 0.0000
             Z scale factor    1.0000


Command:
```

Typical screen report of LIST command after selection of object.

Further activities

Add text to the drawing by creating different text layers and writing labels at heights suitable for different paper sizes.

Read the section about *attributes* in Part 3 of this book. The use of attribute blocks with the drainage symbols could be used to label automatically the components and to keep a list of the number used on the project. Similarly for windows, doors, furniture and any other components.

```
STATUS 300 entities in ACP\SITE
Limits are          X:       0.00      29.00   (Off)
                    Y:       0.00      20.00
Drawing uses        X:       0.00      29.00
                    Y:       0.00      19.00
Display shows       X:      -1.25      14.51
                    Y:       2.14      11.77
Insertion base is   X:       0.00   Y:      0.00   Z:      0.00
Snap resolution is  X:       0.25   Y:      0.25
Grid spacing is     X:       1.00   Y:      1.00

Current layer:     DRAIN
Current color:     BYLAYER -- 7 (white)
Current linetype: DASHED
Current elevation:        0.00  thickness:        0.00
Axis off  Fill off  Grid off  Ortho off  Qtext off  Snap off  Tablet off
Object snap modes: Intersection
Free RAM: 14466 bytes        Free disk: 1495040 bytes
I/O page space:  14K bytes

Command:
```

Typical screen report of STATUS command.

Part Three
AutoCAD Features

This section gives further details of some AutoCAD features which may be useful in producing drawings. The information does not attempt to compete with the AutoCAD reference manual and concentrates on the features likely to be of interest to those people engaged in mainstream drawing activities.

AutoCAD is a large environment and if you want specialised effects then it probably can be done. Read the reference manual – you are probably ready for it now. Most 'special' problems have already been solved by other people who will give or sell you the solution. Look around at the many AutoCAD 'add-on' packages which are available; don't re-invent the wheel!

Part Three
AutoCAD Features

AutoCAD Versions

AutoCAD has sometimes been sold in modules of the *Basic Package*, plus *Advanced Drafting Extensions (ADE)*. Most AutoCAD users now purchase or have access to the complete package and the examples in this book assume that all features are available. The 'basic' AutoCAD package offers most of the powerful drawing and editing features needed for the drawing exercises. The higher-profile enhancements provided by the ADE packages include Dimensioning, Object Snap, Attributes, 3D features and AutoLISP.

The AutoCAD program was first released in 1982 and has evolved through various 'versions' in response to the 'wish lists' of users and to the availability of better equipment. In general, the techniques used in the early versions of AutoCAD, and the drawings produced, can all be used in the later versions. In some cases you need to use the conversion procedure given as an option in the Main Menu. Drawings produced by later versions of AutoCAD, such as Release 9, 10 and onwards *cannot* be used by earlier versions.

Release 9 and higher versions *require* the use of a maths co-processor chip when used with the Intel family of microprocessor chips used in the various IBM and compatible types of computer. Release 9 also introduced a system of pull-down menus, icons and dialogue boxes which supplement the other methods of issuing AutoCAD commands.

Release 10 introduced various viewing enhancements such as split screens and perspective perspective. New 3D capabilities included the ability to draw any entity anywhere in space, with a definable coordinate system to help control the drawing. AutoCAD Release 11 improves various operations, especially those concerning sharing files and networking.

AutoCAD Installation

AutoCAD is a obviously a complex program and because it can run on different computers and different operating systems there are many installation choices. The increased capabilities of computers, networks, displays, plotters and printers gives many more options which need to be fed to AutoCAD at the installation stage.

If you are running AutoCAD on a minicomputer with an operating system such as UNIX then you probably have your own expertise, or access to it. If not, then you shouldn't have the equipment! On a stand-alone PC workstation running PC-DOS, MS-DOS or OS/2, AutoCAD now has the power of earlier minicomputer-based systems and the program comes with a separate Installation Manual with full details.

AutoCAD is installed on a PC system in a fairly standard manner which is within the capabilities of anyone who has installed any of the large modern software packages for microcomputers. AutoCAD supplies an install program which guides you through the procedure. This section offers comments on some of the more common areas of installation on a PC workstation with a hard disk.

Files

The various types of AutoCAD file can be identified by their 3-letter endings or file extensions. These can be seen when you use, for example, the DIR command of DOS.

BAK   backup copy of drawing.
BAS   attribute file in BASIC.
DOC   documentation update to be read.
DRV   driver file for various display and output devices.
DVP   parameter files for devices.
DWG   drawing file with one drawing.
DXB   drawing interchange file in binary format.
DXF   drawing interchange file in AutoCAD format.
EXE   executable files such as the main program *acad.exe*.
HDX   help file with index.
HLP   help file with text.
IGS   drawing interchange file in IGES format.

LIN   linetype file with line information.
LSP   AutoLISP file containing program.
MNU   menu file as originally created.
MNX   compiled menu file after use.
OLD   original version of converted file.
OVL   overlay files containing information which is called by other
             files such as executable files.
PAT   hatch file with patterns.
SCR   script file.
SHX   shape file.
SLB   slide library file containing slides.
SLD   slide drawing file.
$$$ temporary drawing file.
$AC   temporary drawing file.
$RF   current working file.

Directories

AutoCAD makes full use of tree-structured subdirectories and pathnames. All the AutoCAD program files must be kept together in one subdirectory, such as one named *acad*. The drawing files can also be kept in the same subdirectory although it becomes difficult to sort files from such a large number.

If the operating system *path* command contains the name of the subdirectory containing the AutoCAD program files then AutoCAD can be summoned while in another directory. The path command is commonly set by a line in your *autoexec.bat* file which you can change with a text editor.

With a path command in operation you can keep drawings in different subdirectories, such as for different jobs. Use the Change Directory command to make that subdirectory current and then invoke AutoCAD in the usual way, as in the following example:

```
>CD\WORK\HOUSE
>ACAD
```

You can also specify drive names such as A:, and pathnames such as in \WORK\HOUSE\DRAWING1, to refer to files outside of the current directory.

Multiple configurations

You may want to keep several 'types' of AutoCAD which are configured for different equipment, such as one for a mouse and one for a digitiser tablet. When you configure AutoCAD you enter information about your particular equipment which is kept in the configuration file named 'acad.cfd'.

On startup, AutoCAD reads the 'cfg' file which is normally in the same directory as the AutoCAD program files. You can use the SET command of DOS to specify an environment variable ACADCFG whose name is the same as another directory. For example:

C>SET ACADCFG=C:\MOUSE\CFG

will cause AutoCAD to look in the directory called \MOUSE\CFG for the configuration file. To create the configuration file you use the SET command from the operating system and load AutoCAD which then creates a new 'acad.cfg' in that directory. Repeat the process for different directories with different devices in the configuration.

Memory

In the PC/AT range of machines AutoCAD makes use of both 'extended' memory and 'expanded' memory, if they are installed. Expanded memory is usually used first, but the use of both types of memory can be controlled by the following environmental variables activated by the SET command of the operation system.

Extended memory

AutoCAD will use all that extended memory not in use by a RAM disk (VDISK) unless you use a DOS command like the following examples.

>SET ACADXMEM=NONE
>SET ACADXMEM=,*nnn*k   where nnn is the size of the allocated memory in kilobytes.

Expanded memory

AutoCAD will use all the available expanded memory unless you use a DOS command like the following examples.

>SET ACADLIMEM=NONE
>SET ACADLIMEM=*nnn*K   where nnn is the size of the allocated memory in kilobytes.
>SET ACADLIMEM=*nn*   where nn is the number of memory pages to be used.

Plotting

The eventual aim of most AutoCAD drawing sessions is to get results onto paper and the general procedure is given in the Plotting and Printing Prompt page in Part One of the book. The exact procedure depends on the size of your drawing, the size of your paper and the behaviour of your pen plotter or graphics printer. Inevitably you must explore some of these effects by yourself.

AutoCAD needs to know what type of plotter (using pens) or printer (using dot matrix or laser) is being used so that it can send the drawing details in the correct format. You supply this information by choosing from configuration lists during installation. If your particular model of plotter or printer is not listed under its own name then try another model by the same manufacturer. If the manufacturer is not listed then try Hewlett-Packard for pen plotters, Epson for dot matrix printers and Hewlett-Packard for laser printers.

Size and scale

The earlier Plotting and Printing Prompt page described the main options of the PLOT and PRPLOT commands. For metric drawing and A-sized paper (DIN) you should always work in millimetres. You can choose any portion of the drawing for plotting and a simple option is to allow your chosen area of drawing to be 'scaled to fit the available area' on the paper.

Otherwise you must now consider, maybe for the first time, the real size of your lines on a piece of paper. AutoCAD asks for the plot scale in the form of

plotted units (on paper) = *drawing units* (on screen).

An entry of *20=1*, for example, means you want 20 mm on paper to represent 1 drawing unit on screen. Only you can know the meaning of your drawing unit on screen and these can change from drawing to drawing. If one drawing unit represents 1 metre, as in some of our exercises, then the above entry means a scale of 20 mm to 1000 mm. Dividing each figure by 20 shows that this is the same as an architectural scale of 1:50.

In plotting and scaling, trials are worth dozens of words. You can always abort a plot by using Ctrl-C. If the printer has a large memory then you may need to purge it by using the off switch. When you have found settings that suit your routines, make a note of them.

Pens

The output menus for plotters usually have additional menus concerned with pen colours, line types produced by the pens, and software-controlled pen speeds. In Part One of the book, the Prompt pages about Layers and Entities describe how each entity or layer can have a standard colour associated with it.

The plot command option lists the entity colours against the pen numbers in your make of plotter. If necessary you should physically move the pens about in their holder so that the two lists coincide. The 'Linetype' option for the plotter is usually best left as continuous, the default, as the AutoCAD software will handle any discontinuous lines you have used in your drawing.

You also have the opportunity to adjust the 'pen speed'. AutoCAD normally uses the fastest setting for your model of plotter but you can decrease the speed of some or all of the pens if you find that they 'skip' when moved too fast.

The 'Pen width' option affects the efficiency of AutoCAD when it fills a Solid, wide Polyline or Trace. The 'area fill adjustment' option retracts the boundaries of a filled area by one half pen width, an effect which is only needed for high accuracy.

Hatch Patterns

AutoCAD supplies a set of standard hatch patterns which are contained within the *acad.pat* file. Hatch patterns are stored in ASCII format which can be created by using a text editor, such as WordStar in Non-document mode. These files need to be labelled with a *filename.pat* format.

A hatch pattern file has the following two line format.

*name [,description]
angle, x-origin, y-origin, delta-x, delta-y, [,dash-1, dash-2,..]

The description is optional and if the description is omitted no comma is needed. Delta-y is the perpendicular spacing between pattern lines; delta-x is the spacing in the direction of the lines and is applicable to dashed lines. The pattern of a dashed line is specified by optional dash length items where a dash length of zero draws a dot and a negative length indicates a 'pen up' segment which won't be drawn.

The following example is given in the AutoCAD manual:

*L45, 45 degree lines
45,   0, 0   0, 0.5

The above example specifies that the lines are drawn at an angle of 45 degrees. The first line of the pattern passes through the drawing origin (0, 0) and the spacing between the hatch lines of the family is 0.5 drawing units.

ANGLE	ANSI31	ANSI32
ANSI33	ANSI34	ANSI35
ANSI36	ANSI37	ANSI38

BOX	BRASS	BRICK
CLAY	CORK	CROSS
DASH	DOLMIT	DOTS

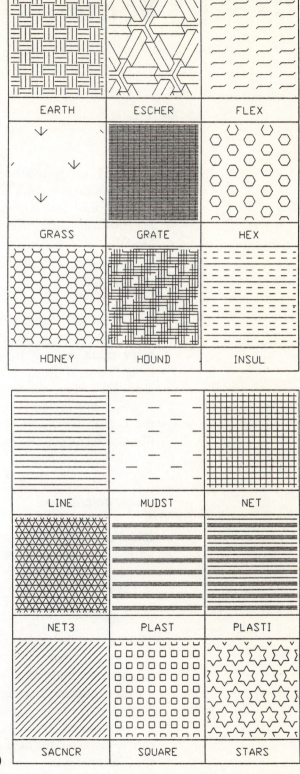

Standard hatch patterns. (Courtesy: Autodesk Ltd.)

Fonts

AutoCAD can generate text in various styles of characters, called fonts, which can be stretched, compressed, rotated and placed anywhere in a drawing. Each font is stored as a separate disk file labelled *fontname.shx*. A file with an '.shx' suffix is a compiled version of *shape* file which has an '.shp' filename suffix.

Shape files

An AutoCAD *shape* is a special entity made up of lines, arc and circle. Shape files are efficient for AutoCAD to store and generate but, being more difficult to use than *blocks*, are not normally used for components of drawings. AutoCAD text fonts are stored in a form of shape file and are the most common application of shapes.

Before a set of shapes can be used in a drawing they must be loaded with the LOAD command. The compiled form of shape file with a 'shx' filename suffix must be used with the LOAD command. The Main Menu has an option to compile shape files.

Shape descriptions

Initial shape files are stored in ASCII format which can be created by using a text editor, such as WordStar in Non-document mode. These files need to be labelled with a 'shp' filename suffix.

The first line of a shape definition has the form:

*shapenumber, defbytes, shapename

This line is followed by one or more lines containing specification bytes separated by commas and ending with a 0. If numbers have a leading zero then they are interpreted as hexadecimal. Every shape in a shape file has a unique number between 1 and 255. Text fonts need specific numbers corresponding to the standard ASCII codes for each character.

The standard AutoCAD files contain some example 'shp' files which can be inspected for their content and the AutoCAD manual should be used for reference.

Fast fonts

txt	The quick brown fox jumps over the lazy dog. ABC123
monotxt	The quick brown fox jumps over the lazy dog. ABC123

Simplex fonts

romans	The quick brown fox jumps over the lazy dog. ABC123
scripts	*The quick brown fox jumps over the lazy dog. ABC123*
greeks	Τηε θυιχκ βροων φοξ δυμπσ ο∈ερ τηε λαζψ δογ. ABX123

Duplex font

romand	The quick brown fox jumps over the lazy dog. ABC123

Complex fonts

romanc	The quick brown fox jumps over the lazy dog. ABC123
italicc	*The quick brown fox jumps over the lazy dog. ABC123*
scriptc	*The quick brown fox jumps over the lazy dog. ABC123*
greekc	Τηε θυιχκ βροων φοξ δυμπσ ο∈ερ τηε λαζψ δογ. ABX123
cyrillic	Узд рфивк бсоцн еоч йфмпт охдс узд лащш гож. АББ123
cyriltlc	Тхе цуичк брошн фож щумпс овер тхе лазй дог. АБЧ123

Triplex fonts

romant	The quick brown fox jumps over the lazy dog. ABC123
italict	*The quick brown fox jumps over the lazy dog. ABC123*

Gothic fonts

gothice	The quick brown fox jumps over the lazy dog. ABC123
gothicg	The quick brown fox jumps over the lazy dog. ABC123
gothici	The quick brown fox jumps over the lazy dog. ABC123

Standard fonts. (Courtesy: Autodesk Ltd.)

Dimensioning

The dimensioning abilities of AutoCAD provide more options and adaptability than can be shown in the drawing examples. This section summarises the special dimensioning commands and variables.

Dimensioning commands

ALIGNED	gives a dimension line parallel to the origins of the extension line.
ANGULAR	gives a dimension arc to show the angle between two non-parallel lines.
BASELINE	continues an offset dimension line from the baseline (first extension line) of the previous dimension.
CENTRE	gives a centre line or centre mark for a circle or an arc.
CONTINUE	continues a dimension line from the second extension line of the previous dimension.
DIAMETER	gives a dimension line across the diameter of a circle or an arc.
EXIT	returns to the normal command mode.
HOMETEXT	restores text to its default location.
HORIZONTAL	gives a horizontal dimension line.
LEADER	gives a line or sequence of lines which allows control over the location of the dimension text.
NEWTEXT	changes the text of existing dimensions.
RADIUS	gives a dimension line across the radius of a circle or arc, with an optional centre mark.
REDRAW	redraws complete display and removes any marks on the drawing.
ROTATED	gives a dimension line at a specified angle.
STATUS	gives a list of all dimensioning variables and their current settings.
STYLE	changes to a new text style for the dimension text.
UNDO	erases the result of the most recent dimensioning command.

UPDATE   updates dimension entities to current setting of the
                      dimension variables.

VERTICAL   gives a vertical dimension line.

Dimensioning variables

The particular manner in which dimensions are drawn depends on a set of
dimensioning variables whose effects are summarised below. Some of the
variables are simple on/off switches.

DIMSE1   Suppress Extension Line 1. Suppresses creation of the
                      first extension line, if set on. Default value is off.

DIMSE2   Suppress Extension Line 2. Suppresses creation of the
                      second extension line if on. Default value is off.

DIMTIH   Text Inside Horizontal. Always draws the text
                      horizontally if set on (the default). If off, the text
                      rotation angle is the same as the angle of the
                      dimension line.

DIMTOH   Text Outside Horizontal. Same effect as DIMTIH
                      but applies to text drawn outside extension lines.

DIMTAD   Text Above Dimension line. Controls the placement
                      of text for linear dimensioning. Text is drawn
                      centred along the dimension line if set off (the
                      default). If set on, the text is placed above the
                      dimension line.

DIMTOL   Tolerance. Adds dimension tolerances to the text if
                      set on. Default value is off.

DIMLIM   Limits. Gives dimension limits as the text if set on.
                      Default value is off.

DIMALT   Alternate units. Allows dimensioning in alternate
                      units if set on. Default value is off.

DIMASO   Associative dimensioning. Gives associative
                      dimension entities when set to on (the default).
                      When set off, the parts of a dimension are drawn
                      as separate entities.

DIMSHO   Show new dimension. Re-computes associative
                      dimensions as they are dragged if DIMSHO set on.
                      If set off (the default) the dragging process is faster
                      on some computers.

DIMASZ   Arrow Size. Specifies the size of arrows at the ends of
                      dimension lines. Default value is 0.18 units.

DIMTSZ   Tick Size. Specifies the size of the dimension ticks
                      used instead of arrows. Arrows are drawn if set to
                      zero (the default).

DIMTXT	Text size. Specifies the height of dimension text. Default value is 0.18 units.
DIMCEN	Centre mark size. Controls the marks and lines at the centres of circles and arcs. Gives the size of the mark if greater than zero (default value = 0.09 units). If zero, marks or lines are not drawn. If negative, centre lines are drawn rather centre marks.
DIMEXO	Extension line Offset. Specifies the distance between the origin points and the extension lines. Default value = 0.0628 units.
DIMEXE	Extension line Extension. Specifies the extension of the extension line beyond the dimension line. Default value = 0 units.
DIMDLE	Dimension line Extension. Specifies the extension of the dimension line past the extension line if DIMSTZ is also nonzero. Default value = 0 units.
DIMDLI	Dimension line Increment. Specifies the offset for successive continuations when continuation is used. Default value = 0.38 units.
DIMTP	Plus tolerance. Default value = 0 units.
DIMTM	Minus toerance. Default value = 0 units.
DIMRND	Rounding value. Used for rounding of all dimensioning distances. Default value = 0 (no rounding).
DIMSCALE	sets the overall scale factor applied to all dimensioning variables with sizes, distances or offsets. Default value = 1.0.
DIMLFAC	Length Factor. Used as a global scale factor for linear dimensioning. Default value = 1.0.
DIMALTF	Alternate units Factor. Sets a value if the associated DIMALT variable is set on. Default value = 25.4 (mm to the inch).
DIMALTD	Alternate units Decimal places. Set the number of decimal places in the alternate units. Default value = 2.
DIMZIN	controls the editing of the 'inches' part of a feet and inches distance. Default value = 0. A common value is 3 to include precisely zero inches.
DIMPOST	defines a character string to be edited after the dimension measurement, such as mm. Default value: no suffix.
DIMAPOST	defines a character string to be edited after an alternate dimensioning measurement (except for angular dimensions.) Default value = no suffix.

DIMBLK   gives the name of block to be drawn instead of
                   normal arrow or ticks on dimension lines. Default
                   value = none.

Associative dimensioning

Associate dimension entities automatically change their values when you
edit objects within the drawing. The following commands can operate on
associative dimensions:

ARRAY, EXTEND, MIRROR, ROTATE, SCALE,
STRETCH, TRIM.

The definition points of the dimension entity must be included in the
objects selected for the editing operation.

Definition points are points drawn at the places used to create an
associative dimension entity. In general these points are end points or
intersection points of lines within the dimension system. To be sure of
including all definition points you should select objects with the Window
or the Crossing option.

TABLET Operation

A digitising tablet is a device used to give input to AutoCAD, like a keyboard or mouse. The tablet is an electronic board on which a *stylus* or *puck* pointing device is moved about causing the crosshairs to move on screen. Unlike a mouse, the stylus knows where it is in relation to the board and the board can therefore contain information such as a menu or another drawing.

Tablet menus use a digitising tablet by setting aside rectangular areas for the entry of AutoCAD commands. Menu forms with printed icons are fixed onto the board to help you pick as appropriate command with the pointing device. These menus on the digitiser are linked to the AutoCAD program by using the TABLET.CFG command of AutoCAD.

Another use of a tablet is to trace or *digitise* an existing paper drawing by fixing the drawing onto the tablet. As the pointing device is moved between points on the paper drawing the crosshairs move across the screen. Normal AutoCAD drawing commands are given and when points are called they are picked from the drawing on the tablet.

The TABLET command includes an option to calibrate the scale of the original paper drawing against the screen copy. Two known points on the paper are picked and their coordinates are entered via the keyboard. If the paper drawing is too large to fit onto the tablet then you can digitise it in sections and assemble them later.

A tablet can only provide a two-dimensional input with x and y coordinates. The z coordinate for each point is taken to be that of the current value. This value can be changed just before the digitising of any point by changing the UCS (User Coordinate System).

Digitised objects will not be as accurate as objects created with AutoCAD entities because the AutoCAD drawing aids are far more accurate than the eye or the ruler. Fortunately, the Snap and Ortho settings can be used while digitising. To 'clean up' a digitised drawing you can adjust points with the CHANGE or CHPROP commands and use aids such as OSNAP settings and the FILLET command.

Sketching

The SKETCH command allows you to enter a freehand drawing into an AutoCAD drawing. As you move the pointing device, such as a mouse, the cursor immediately makes the same path on screen. This freehand 'trace' is actually constructed from a connected series of lines.

Be warned that just a short sketched line can create as many lines, to AutoCAD, as a large 'normal' drawing and sketching therefore occupies a lot of space on your disk. Before using the SKETCH command you should use the STATUS command to check that you have enough memory available.

SKETCH uses the idea of a an imaginary pen which produces sketches on screen when you set it 'down' on the paper and stops when you set it 'up' off the paper. Sketched lines can be edited like other lines and grouped together as blocks.

The accuracy or resolution of a sketch depends on the increment which you can enter at the start of the command. An increment of 0.1 drawing units is typical. The SKETCH command then offers the the following subcommands:

Pen up/down	P. Lifts the sketching pen (if down) or lowers pen (if up).
Line to point	'.' Entering a full-stop draws a straight line from the endpoint of last sketched line to the current location.
Record	R. Records all sketched lines as permanent lines which then behave as AutoCAD entities.
Record & Exit	X. Records all sketched lines and returns to normal AutoCAD command prompt.
Quit	Q. Discards all lines sketched since start of SKETCH command or last R command.
Erase	E. Allows erasure of portion of sketched line which is not yet recorded. Pick appropriate point back from end point.
Connect	C. Connects to endpoint of last line after pen has been raised.

SKETCH effects

Sketch lines are not added to the drawing until you record them or exit the

SKETCH command. The temporary sketch lines are displayed in a different screen colour. If AutoCAD detects that it is running out of computer memory to store the temporary lines it will bleep and ask you to 'raise the pen' while it uses the memory on disk.

If you are sketching with a small increment on a relatively slow computer then it is possible for the computer to be still doing the calculations for one point as you pass the next point. The details of that next point will be lost unless you slow down the speed of your pointer.

With a digitising tablet you can use the *Tablet mode* to sketch information from a paper drawing. You cannot point to the screen menu from the digitiser but that menu area of the digitiser can be used for drawing. Sketching while in Tablet mode requires AutoCAD to do more calculations than in screen mode so you may need to trace more slowly in order to preserve accuracy. When following some movements on the tablet the crosshairs on screen may disappear and you should use the ZOOM command to see the desired area.

Snap mode can be used while sketching and the snap points will override any smaller increments.

When *Ortho mode* is set to on, the SKETCH command will only draw vertical or horizontal lines. A diagonal line will be converted to a series of horizontal and vertical lines with a 'staircase' effect.

Menus

The menus which you use to select AutoCAD commands can be changed to suit your working practices or to present options to a inexperienced user. For example, you might wish to rearrange the order of the AutoCAD commands. To make a customised menu you need to have a good knowledge of AutoCAD commands and their various options.

When AutoCAD opens a drawing file it looks for and loads the standard menu file called *acad.mnx*. The prompt line at the bottom of the screen reports the successful loading of the menu. You can load an alternative menu by giving the MENU command and typing the name of the new menu.

All the menus used by AutoCAD are initially created as plain text ASCII files with the filename ending of '.mnu'. These files are written with a plain text editor, such as WordStar in 'Non-document mode'. When AutoCAD first encounters a .mnu file it compiles it into a new file with the same name but with a filename ending of '.mnx'. The compiled form of menu file is more compact and can be loaded more quickly.

A menu file consists of a list of AutoCAD commands with parameters, and some special symbols which activate AutoCAD effects, such as in the following simple example.

```
***SCREEN
[CLOSEUP] ^ C ^ Czoom E
[FARVIEW] ^ C ^ Czoom L
```

Each item must be on a separate line, with spaces as shown. Special symbols include the following:

[title]	displays as a menu title.
**name	starts a submenu.
$S=	displays another submenu.
^C	cancels.
^B	Snap mode on/off.
^O	Ortho mode on/off.
^G	Grid mode on/off.
^D	Coordinate display on/off.
^E	Isoplane left/top/right.
^T	Tablet mode on/off.
;	acts as RETURN.
\	pauses for input.

Attributes

Attributes are a special form of AutoCAD entity or block which contains text information. This information, which is automatically updated as you change a drawing, can be exported for use in databases, spreadsheets and word processors. Attributes can also be used on drawings instead of the TEXT command, especially where you often use labels which vary only slightly.

Creating Attributes

The ATTDEF command creates an Attribute definition which acts as a template for the Attribute. The command is used to specify the 'tag' or description of the Attribute and the actual 'value' of the information.

There are four types of Attribute *mode* which are switched on/off by entering 'Y' or 'N' and pressing RETURN to accept the final settings:

Invisible   I. Suppresses the display of the Attribute value when the Attribute block is inserted.

Constant   C. Gives the Attribute a fixed value for all insertions.

Verify   V. Offers a chance during insertion to verify that the value is correct.

Preset   P. Allows the creation of variable Attributes which are not requested when the Attribute block is inserted.

The ATTDEF command prompts you to enter the Attribute tag (heading) and the Attribute value (contents). You then specify the position and size of the information text, which is usually placed on or alongside the appropriate object on screen. A standard value can be entered as the default for the Attribute value or it can be left as nul. Pressing RETURN or the space bar repeats the ATTDEF command so that further tags and values can be defined.

The BLOCK command is used to save the Attribute using a window to select both the drawing and the Attribute texts. The INSERT command is used to recall the block and after the usual prompts for scale and rotation factors, you are also prompted for the 'Attribute values'. You can then enter a particular label for the object being inserted. If you press RETURN then the 'tag' or heading will be used for the text.

In the following simple example of kitchen units, the shape is drawn on screen then the ATTDEF command is used. The first Attribute tag is 'UNIT TYPE' which can also act as the prompt. The second Attribute tag is 'SIZE' and the third tag is 'CODE'. The BLOCK command is used to save these tags, along with the drawing, using a block name like UNIT.

UNIT TYPE	SIZE	CODE
Base Unit	500	B5
Wall Unit	500	W5

The INSERT command is repeatedly used to recall the block and to enter the Attribute values such as 'Base Unit', '500' and 'B5'. If you don't enter values then the tags (UNIT TYPE, SIZE or CODE) are used for the text.

The ATTDISP command is used to inspect all Attributes, even if they were defined with the Invisible mode on.

Editing Attributes

The ATTEDIT command allows you to edit Attributes one at a time or to make a global changes to a set of Attributes. For both types of editing mode you need to select the Attributes to be edited and all Attributes can be selected by specified Block names, Attribute tags, or Attribute values.

For *global editing* the display screen flips to the text mode. When prompted, you enter the contents of 'string' (length of text) that you wish to change and the contents of the new version. AutoCAD then examines the selected Attributes and makes the replacement where appropriate. Beware of unexpected replacements if the strings are short.

For *individual editing* you can also select Attributes by the usual selection tools such as by pointing or windowing. You are given the option of changing the value of an Attribute by editing the string, as for the global change, or by making a complete new entry. Other Attribute properties which can be changed are position, text height, text angle, text style, layer, or colour.

Extracting Attributes

The ATTEXT command retrieves Attribute information from a drawing and writes it to a disk file in various formats suitable for analysis and use by other programs such as a database.

The ATTEXT command gives you the following options:

Entities   E. Allows you to select the objects whose Attributes are to be extracted.

CDF   Comma Delimited Format is the default format. This format can be read directly by packages such as dBaseIII/IV and is easily handled by programs written in BASIC.

SDF   This format is also recognised by many packages such as databases and spreadsheets and is easily handled by programs written in FORTRAN.

DXF   This format is a variation of AutoCAD's own Drawing Interchange File format.

The extract *filename* is asked for, otherwise the drawing filename is used. The filename ending will be '.txt' for CDF and SDF formats and '.dxx' for DXF format. With MS/PC-DOS systems, instead of a filename you can use CON to direct output to the screen or PRN to send information to the printer.

A *template file* can be used to structure the extract file by specifying which Attributes are to be included and how the information is to be presented. A template file can be created with an plain text (ASCII) text editor using a file ending of '.txt'.Each line of the template specifies one field name, its character width, and its numerical precision if applicable.

The following template file refers to the previous example of kitchen units.

UNIT TYPE C012000
SIZE N006004
CODE C006000

The first C*wwwddd* specifies a character field with a width of 12 characters and no decimal places. The N*wwwddd* entry specifies a numeric type of field with a width of 6 characters and 4 decimal places.

Information about the block entities can also be extracted using the following codes:

BL:LEVEL   Nwww000   for Block nesting level.
BL:NAME   Cwww000   for Block name.
BL:X   Nwwwddd   for X coordinate of Block.
BL:Y   Nwwwddd   for Y coordinate of Block.
BL:LAYER   Cwww000   for Block insertion layer.
BL:ORIENT   Nwwwddd   for Block rotation angle.
BL:XSCALE   Nwwwddd   for X scale factor of Block.
BL:YSCALE   Nwwwddd   for Y scale factor of Block.

Command Scripts

The *script* feature of AutoCAD allows it to read a sequence of commands from a text file. A script can be used to create a automated demonstration showing any sequence of AutoCAD techniques and also be combined with the *slide* capability described separately. The SCRIPT facility includes has some special rules and commands described below.

Script file

You create the script file outside of AutoCAD using a 'text editor' which creates a plain text (ASCII) file. The 'programmer' mode of word processors such as WordStar (Non-document mode), or utilities such as SideKick are suitable. Do not use the ordinary mode of your word processor as it probably adds formatting codes, even if you can't see them.

The filename must be given the suffix '.scr' such as in *demo1.scr*. Each line of the script file contains a response in that would enter on the AutoCAD prompt line at the bottom of the screen. You must start a new line for each command or option and carefully use blank spaces or lines instead of RETURN (because the space key is an alternative to the RETURN key).

The following example sequence is designed to start at the Main Menu:

Entry	Comment
1	to choose new drawing option.
box	as drawing name.
line 1, 1 1, 5 5, 5 5, 1 c	to draw box.
delay 6000	to pause six seconds.
quit y	to abandon.

Starting

A script file can be invoked when AutoCAD is loaded from the operating system DOS command. The script file must be the second file named after the acad program file, as in the following example:

C>*acad drawing1 demo1*

The first lines of the script need to give the appropriate responses to the Main Menu prompts. If the script gives a different drawing name then the latter will be used.

SCRIPT

The SCRIPT command calls up a previously-saved script file and executes the sequence of commands in the file. The SCRIPT command is given at the 'command' prompt inside AutoCAD as follows:

Command: *SCRIPT* Script file: *filename*

You enter the filename of your pre-prepared script file, but the '.scr' suffix of the filename is not entered. When the sequence of stored commands has been executed the command prompt reappears.

DELAY

The DELAY command gives a pause in the script sequence, which is useful to allow people to see details of operations which happen quickly on screen.

Command: *DELAY* Delay time in milliseconds: *number*

There are 1000 milliseconds in a second so that entering *DELAY 1000* pauses operations for a time of the order of 1 second. The exact time will depend on the processing speed of your machine and you may need to experiment. The maximum number that you can enter is 32767.

RESUME

The RESUME command continues the running of an interrupted script. Scripts can be interrupted by pressing **Ctrl C** or the **Backspace** key and other commands can be entered. The RESUME command can also be given within the middle of a command by entering '*RESUME*.

GRAPHSCR, TEXTSCR

The GRAPHSCR and TEXTSCR commands flip the display screen between the text mode used for information such as help and the graphics mode used for drawing. This would normally be done manually such as by using the function key F1. The commands are ignored on dual-screen systems.

RSCRIPT

The RSCRIPT command causes the script to repeat. RSCRIPT is not understood in the Main Menu so it must be entered before an END or QUIT Y command in the script.

AutoCAD Commands

The following list of AutoCAD commands summarises their effects. A 'transparent command', prefixed by an apostrophe (') in menus, is a command that can be used while within the options of another command. Dimensioning commands are summarised in a separate section.

APERTURE	controls the size of the target box for object snap operations.
ARC	creates curves made from part of circle.
AREA	calculates the area of a figure with a continuous boundary.
ARRAY	makes multiple copies of selected objects in a rectangular or circular pattern.
ATTDEF	creates an Attribute Definition entity which allows text information to be stored with a Block Definition.
ATTDISP	controls the visibility of Attribute entities.
ATTEDIT	allows editing of Attributes.
ATTEXT	Extracts Attribute data from a drawing.
AXIS	displays ruler lines along the edges of the screen.
BASE	specifies an origin for insertion into another drawing.
BLIPMODE	controls display of marker blips on screen.
BLOCK	makes a compound object from a group of separate entities.
BREAK	erases part of an object, or splits it into two.
CHAMFER	creates a flattened corner at an intersection.
CHANGE	changes position, size and other properties of selected objects.
CHPROP	changes properties of selected properties.
CIRCLE	forms a circle of any size.
COLOUR	sets the colour for all subsequent objects.
COPY	makes a copy of selected objects.
DBLIST	lists information for all entities in the drawing.
DDATTE	uses a dialogue box to edit Attributes.
DDEMODES	uses a dialogue box to set current layer, colour, linetype, elevation and thickness (Transparent command).

DDLMODES	uses a dialogue box to set layer properties (Transparent command).
DDRMODES	uses a dialogue box to set drawing aids (Transparent command).
DELAY	delays execution of the following command.
DIM	starts dimensioning mode and allows many dimensions to be entered.
DIM1	allows one dimension to be entered and returns to normal command mode.
DIST	calculates the distance between any two points.
DIVIDE	places markers on a selected object which divide the object into a chosen number of equal parts.
DOUGHNUT or DONUT	forms a filled circle or ring.
DRAGMODE	controls the 'dragging' mode which operates for some commands.
DTEXT	draws text characters 'dynamically' as soon as they are entered.
DVIEW	defines parallel or visual perspective views.
DXBIN	inserts binary files into a drawing.
DXFIN	loads a DXF drawing interchange file.
DXFOUT	creates a DXF drawing interchange file.
GESURF	creates a 3D polygon mesh which approximates a Coons surface patch.
ELEV	sets the elevation (base) and thickness (height) for all subsequent objects. Used for 3D visualisations.
ELLIPSE	forms an ellipse with a choice of methods.
END	saves the drawing to a file and returns to the Main Menu.
ERASE	erases selected items.
EXPLODE	separates a Block or Polyline into constituent parts.
EXTEND	extends a Line, Arc or Polyline to meet another object.
FILES	llows disk file operations.
FILL	controls the fill effect for Solids, Traces, and wide Polylines.
FILLET	makes a sharp or curved join between two lines, arcs or circles.
FILMROLL	creates a file for use by AutoShade.
GRAPHSCR	in a command script, switches screen display to graphics mode (Transparent command).
GRID	displays a grid of dots on screen at specified spacing.

HANDLES	assigns a unique reference number to each entity.
HATCH	fills specified areas with chosen patterns.
HELP or ?	displays a list of commands and options or supplies help about a specific command (Transparent command).
HIDE	removes 'hidden' lines from a 3D visualisation.
ID	gives the coordinates of a specified point.
IGESIN	loads an IGES interchange file.
IGESOUT	creates an IGES interchange file.
INSERT	inserts into the drawing a copy of a prepared Block or part.
ISOPLANE	selects a plane of an isometric grid.
LAYER	creates and controls drawing layers.
LIMITS	controls the drawing boundaries.
LINE	creates lines of any length.
LINETYPE	controls the continuous/dashed nature of subsequent objects.
LIST	lists information about selected objects.
LOAD	loads a file of prepared Shapes.
LTSCALE	sets the scale factor to be applied to linetypes.
MEASURE	places markers at intervals along a selected object.
MENU	loads the menu areas with a chosen file of commands.
MINSERT	inserts multiple copies of a Block in a rectangular pattern.
MIRROR	makes a reversed copy of an chosen object.
MSLIDE	makes a slide file from the current screen display.
MULTIPLE	repeats the next command until cancelled.
OFFSET	creates an identical curve or line in a parallel position.
OOPS	restores erased objects.
ORTHO	forces all entered lines to be aligned with the grid.
OSNAP	allows points to be accurately located to reference points.
PAN	moves the display screen across the drawing (Tranparent command).
PEDIT(2D)	allows editing of 2D polylines.
PEDIT(3D)	allows editing of 3D polylines.
PEDIT (Mesh)	allows editing of 3D polygon meshes.
PLAN	changes display to PLAN view.
PLINE	creates connected lines and arcs which behave as a single object.
PLOT	plots a drawing using a pen plotter.
POINT	draws single points.

POLYGON	draws polygons with specified number of sides.
PRPLOT	plots a drawing using a printer plotter.
PURGE	removes unused layers, blocks, text styles, or linetypes.
QTEXT	identifies text objects without displaying detail.
QUIT	abandons the drawing without saving and returns to the Main Menu.
REDEFINE	restores a command deleted by UNDEFINE.
REDO	reverses the effect of the U or UNDO command.
REDRAW	refreshes and cleans the current viewport (Transparent command).
REDRAWALL	redraws all viewports (Transparent command).
REGEN	regenerates the current viewport.
REGENALL	regenerates all viewports.
REGENAUTO	controls automatic regeneration.
RENAME	changes the name of layers, blocks, text styles, linetypes and views.
RESUME	resumes an interrupted command script (Transparent command).
REVSURF	creates a 3D polygon mesh which approximates to a surface of revolution by rotating a curve around an axis.
ROTATE	rotates chosen objects.
RSCRIPT	restarts a command script from the beginning.
RULESURF	creates a 3D polygon which approximates to a ruled surface between two curves.
SAVE	saves the drawing to a file without leaving the Drawing Editor.
SCALE	alters the proportions of chosen objects.
SCRIPT	executes a command script.
SELECT	groups objects into a set for operation in subsequent commands.
SETVAR	controls the display or value of system variables (Transparent command).
SH	gives access to PC-DOS/MS-DOS internal commands.
SHAPE	draws pre-defined shapes.
SHELL	gives access to other programs without leaving AutoCAD.
SKETCH	allows free-hand drawing.
SNAP	controls precision of digitiser point entry.
SOLID	draws filled-in polygons.
STATUS	displays information about current drawing.
STRETCH	allows selected parts of a drawing to be stretched.

STYLE	creates user-designed text styles.
TABLET	calibrates the digitiser with the coordinates of a paper.
TABSURF	creates a polygon mesh which approximates a tabulated surface defined by vectors.
TEXT	draws text of chosen style and size.
TEXTSCR	in a command script, switches screen display to text display (Transparent command).
TIME	displays times of drawing creation and updates.
TRACE	creates solid lines with specified widths.
TRIM	erases parts of selected objects which cross a specified boundary.
U	reverses the effect of the previous command.
UCS	defines or changes the current User Coordinate System.
USCICON	controls the User Coordinate System icon.
UNDEFINE	deletes the definition of an AutoCAD command.
UNDO	reverses the effect of multiple commands and controls the undo features.
UNITS	controls the coordinates, angles, precision of the current drawing.
VIEWPORTS or VPORTS	divides graphics screen into areas which can display different views of the same drawing.
VIEW	saves the current screen display as named view. Restores a saved view to the display (Tranparent command).
VIEWRES	controls the speed and precision of circle and arc objects.
VPOINT	controls viewpoint for a 3D visualisation.
VSLIDE	displays a previously-saved slide file.
WBLOCK	saves selected objects to a disk file.
ZOOM	enlarges or reduces the display of the drawing (Tranparent command).
3DFACE	draws plane sections with 3D properties.
3DMESH	defines a 3D polygon mesh.
3DPOLY	creates a 3D polyline.

AutoCAD Variables

The AutoCAD *system variables* are settings and values which can be read and changed (unless read-only) by using the SETVAR command. These variables can also be manipulated by AutoLISP.

The variables may be of the various *types* which are indicated with the abbreviations shown here:

I   Integer number
R   Real number
P   Point coordinates
S   Text string

Many AutoCAD variables are saved within each drawing (indicated by 'dwg') while some others are saved in the general configuration file (indicated by 'cfg').

ACADPREFIX	S. Directory name specified by the AutoCAD environmental variable, with appropriate path separator. Read-only.
ACADVER	S. AutoCAD version number. Read-only.
AFLAGS	I. Attribute flags bit-code for ATTDEG command where 1 = invisible, 2 = constant, 4 = verify, 8 = pre-set.
ANGBASE	R, dwg. Angle 0 direction with respect to current UCS.
ANGDIR	I, dwg. 1 = clockwise angles, 0 = anticlockwise angles. With respect to the current UCS.
APERTURE	I, cfg. Object snap target height, in pixels.
AREA	R. True area computed by AREA, LIST or DBLIST. Read-only.
ATTDIA	I, dwg. 1 = insert command uses dialogue box for entry of attribute values. 0 = issue prompts.
ATTMODE	I, dwg. Attribute display mode where 0 = off, 1 = normal, 2 = on.
ATTREQ	I, dwg. 0 = assume defaults for values of all Attributes during INSERT of Blocks, 1 = enable prompts for Attribute values selected by ATTDIA.

AUNITS	I, dwg. Angular units mode where 0 = decimal degrees, 1 = degrees/minutes/seconds, 2 = grads, 3 = radians, 4 = surveyor's units.
AUPREC	I, dwg. Angular units, decimal places.
AXISMODE	I, dwg. Axis display where 1 = on, 0 = off.
AXISUNIT	2D-P, dwg. Axis spacing, X and Y.
BACKZ	R, dwg. Back clipping plane for current viewport in drawing units.
BLIPMODE	I, dwg. Marker blips where 1 = on, 0 = off.
CDATE	R. Calendar date/time. Read-only.
CECOLOUR	S, dwg. Current entity colour. Read-only.
CELTYPE	S, dwg. Current entity linetype. Read-only.
CHAMFERA	R, dwg. First chamfer distance.
CHAMFERB	R, dwg. Second chamfer distance.
CLAYER	S, dwg. Current layer. Read-only.
CMECHO	I. Echoes AutoLISP prompts and input. 1 = on, 0 = off.
COORDS	I, dwg. 0 = coordinate display updated on point picks only, 1 = absolute coordinate display updated continuously, 2 = distance and angle displayed when requested.
CVPORT	I, dwg. Identification number of current viewport.
DATE	R. Julian date/time. Read-only.
DIMxxx	Assorted types, dwg. All dimensioning variables are also system variables.
DISTANCE	R. Distance calculated by DIST command. Read-only.
DRAGMODE	I, dwg. 0 = no dragging, 1 = on when requested, 2 = auto.
DRAGP1	I, cfg. Regen-drag input sampling rate.
DRAG2	I, cfg. Fast-drag input sampling rate.
DWGNAME	S. User-defined drawing name. Read-only.
DWGPREFIX	S. Drive/directory prefix for drawing. Read-only.
ELEVATION	R, dwg. Current 3D elevation, relative to the current UCS.
EXPERT	I. Controls appearance of 'are you sure' prompts for some commands. 0 = normal, to 4 = suppress all prompts.
EXTMAX	3D-P, dwg. Upper right 'drawing uses' extents.
EXTMIN	3D-P, dwg. Lower left 'drawing uses' extents.
FILLTRAD	R, dwg. Fillet radius.
FILLMODE	I, dwg. Fill mode where 1= on, 0 = off.
FLATLAND	Temporary 3D conversion aid for drawings created before Release 10. 0 = default, 1 = suppress new features.

FRONTZ	R, dwg. Front clipping plane offset for the current viewport, in drawing units.
GRIDMODE	I, dwg. Grid in current viewport where 1 = on, 0 = grid off.
GRIDUNIT	P, dwg. Grid spacing for current viewport.
HANDLES	I, dwg. Entity handles where 0 = disable, 1 = on. Read-only.
HIGHLIGHT	I. Object selection highlighting where 1 = on, 0 = off.
INSBASE	3D-P, dwg. Insertion base point in UCS coordinates.
LASTANGLE	R. End angle of last arc, relative to XY plane of current UCS. Read-only.
LASTPOINT	3D-P. Last point entered, in UCS coordinates. Obtained by entry of '@' from keyboard.
LASTPT3D	3D-P. Same as LASTPOINT.
LENSLENGTH	R, dwg. Length of lens, in mm, for perspective drawing. Read-only.
LIMCHECK	I, dwg. Limits checking, where 1 = on, 0 = off.
LIMMAX	2D-P, dwg. Upper right drawing limits.
LIMMIN	2D-P, dwg. Lower left drawing limits
LTSCALE	R, dwg. Global linetype scale factor.
LUNITS	I, dwg. Linear units mode where 1 = scientific, 2 = decimal, 3 = engineering, 4 = architectural, 5 = fractional.
LUPREC	I, dwg. Linear units decimal places or denominator.
MENUECHO	I. Menu echo/prompt control bits which are sum of the following: 0 = all menu items and prompts displayed (default); 1= suppress echo; 2 = suppress printing of system prompts; 4 disable Ctrl-P toggle of menu item echoing.
MENUNAME	S, dwg. Name of the current menu.
MIRRTEXT	I, dwg. MIRROR command reflects text if non-zero, retains text direction if zero.
ORTHOMODE	I, dwg. Ortho mode where 1 = on, 0 = off.
OSMODE	I, dwg. Object snap modes bit-code which are the sum of the following: 1 = Endpoint; 2 = Midpoint; 4 = Centre; 8 = Node; 16 = Quadrant; 32 = Intersection; 64 = Insertion; 128 = Perpendicular; 256 = Tangent; 512 = Nearest; 1024 = Quick.
PMODE	I, dwg. Point entity display mode.
PDSIZE	R, dwg. Point entity display size.
PERIMETER	R. Perimeter as computed by AREA, LIST or DBLIST. Read-only.

PICKBOX	I, cfg. Height of object selection target box, in pixels.
POPUPS	I. 1 = currently configured display supports dialogue boxes, menu bar, pull-down and icon menus. 0 = previous feature not available. Read-only.
QTEXTMODE	I, dwg. Quick text mode where 1 = on , 0 = off.
REGENMODE	I, dwg. REGENAUTO, where 1 = on, 0 = off.
SCREENSIZE	2D-P. Size of current viewport in pixels. Read-only.
SKETHINC	R, dwg. Sketch record increment.
SKPOLY	I, dwg. Sketch effects, where 1 = polylines, 0 = lines.
SNAPANG	R, dwg. Snap/grid rotation angle (relative to the UCS) for current viewport.
SNAPBASE	2D-P, dwg. Snap/grid origin point for current viewport.
SNAPISOPAIR	I, dwg. Current isometric plane for current viewport where 0 = left, 1 = top, 2 = right.
SNAPMODE	I, dwg. Snap mode for current viewport where 1 = on, 0 = off.
SNAPSTYL	I, dwg. Snap style for current viewport where 0 = standard, 1 = isometric.
SNAPUNIT	2D-P, dwg. Snap spacing for current viewport, X and Y.
SPLFRAME	I, dwg. If variable = 1 then the following effects: the control polygon for spline fit Polylines is displayed; only the defining mesh of a surface fit Polygon is displayed; invisible edges of 3D Faces are displayed.
	If variable = 0 the the following effects: control polygon for spline fit Polylines not displayed; fit surface of a polygon mesh displayed; invisible edges of 3D Faces not displayed.
SPLINESEGES	I, dwg. Number of line segments generated for spline patch.
SPLINETYPE	I, dwg. Type of spline curve generated by PEDIT where 5 = quadratic B-spline, 6 = cubic B-spline.
SURFTAB1	I, dwg. Number of tabulations generated for RULESURF and TABSURF commands. Also mesh density in M direction for REVSURF and EDGESURF.
SURFTAB2	I, dwg. Mesh density in N direction for REVSURF and EDGESURF.

SURFTYPE	I, dwg. Type of surface fitting performed by PEDIT where 5 = quadratic B-spline surface, 6 = cubic B-spline surface, 8 = Bezier surface.
SURFU	I, dwg. Surface density in M direction.
SURFV	I, dwg. Surface density in N direction.
TARGET	3D-P, dwg. UCS location of target point for current viewport. Read-only.
TDCREATE	R, dwg. Time and date of drawing creation. Read-only.
TDINDWG	R, dwg. Total editing time. Read-only.
TDUPDATE	R, dwg. Time and date of last update. Read-only.
TDUSRTIMER	R, DWG. User elapsed timer. Read-only.
TEMPPREFIX	S. Contains directory name configured for temporary files.
TEXTEVAL	I. If variable = 0 then all responses to prompts for string text and attribute values are literal. If variable = 1 then text starting with '(' or '!' is taken to be an AutoLISP expression.
TEXTSIZE	R, dwg. Default height for new text entities drawn with current text style.
TEXTSTYLE	S, dwg. Contains name of current text style. Read-only.
THICKNESS	R, dwg. Current 3D thickness.
TRACEWID	R, dwg. Default trace width.
UCSFOLLOW	I, dwg. I variable = 1 then any UCS change gives an automatic change to plan view of the new UCS. If variable = 0 a UCS change doesn't affect view.
UCSICON	I, dwg. Coordinate system icon bit-mode which is sum following: 1 = on, 2 = origin.
UCSNAME	S, dwg. Name of current coordinate system.
UCSORG	3D-P, dwg. Origin point of current coordinate system given in World coordinates. Read-only.
UCSXDIR	3D-P, dwg. The X-direction of current UCS. Read-only.
UCSYDIR	3D-P, dwg. The Y-direction of current UCS. Read-only.
USERI1-5	I, dwg. Five variables for storage and retrieval of integer values.
USERR1-5	R, dwg. Five variables for storage and retrieval of real numbers.
VIEWCTR	3D-P, dwg. Centre of view in current viewport, in UCS coordinates. Read-only.
VIEWDIR	3D-P, dwg. Viewing direction of current viewport. Read-only.

VIEWMODE	I, dwg. Viewing mode bit-code for current viewport which is sum of following: 1 = perspective view, 2 = front clipping on, 4 = back clipping on, 8 = UCS follow mode on, 16 = frontclip not at eye.
VIEWSIZE	R, dwg. Height of current view, in drawing units. Read-only.
VIEWTWIST	R, dwg. Twist angle for current view. Read-only.
VPOINTX, VPOINTY, VPOINTZ	R, dwg. X, Y, and Z components for direction of current viewport. Similar to VIEWDIR.
VSMAX	3D-P. Upper right corner for virtual screen of the current viewport. Read-only.
VSMIN	3D-P. Lower left corner for virtual screen of the current viewport. Read-only.
WORLDUCS	I. If variable = 1, current UCS is same as World Coordinate System. If = 0, it is not. Read-only.
WORLDVIEW	I, dwg. DVIEW and VPOINT command relative to the current UCS. If variable = 1, then current UCS changed to WCS. Default = 0.

AutoLISP

AutoLISP is a programming language which works within AutoCAD and is commonly used by developers who write specialised applications for AutoCAD users. AutoLISP is a form of the LISP programming language and the AutoLISP Programmer's Reference, supplied with the AutoCAD package, contains further information to help achieve effective programming.

You can also use AutoLISP to write automatic sequences or 'macros' that produce powerful AutoCAD effects with simple commands. If you often use a certain sequence of AutoCAD manoeuvres, such as creating a door opening, then the procedure can be automated by AutoLISP.

AutoLISP procedures can also be used to control AutoCAD menus and options. The standard AutoCAD menu includes some AutoLISP routines for 'SETUP' or for drawing 3D objects and you can inspect the '.LSP' files for these routines.

AutoLISP Expressions

Each AutoLISP expression begins with an opening bracket, a function name, an optional list of arguments and a closing bracket in the following form.

  (function name [arguments]...)

A *function* is a ready-made instruction which tells AutoLISP what to do and an *argument* is the information which is processed by the function. An arguments can be a label, a number or a list. An AutoLISP expression like the above results in a value which is 'returned' for use by AutoCAD. An AutoLISP expression can itself be 'nested' inside another expression before producing the value.

You can type an AutoLISP expression at the AutoCAD prompt and the value of the expression is displayed. The prompt sign changes but another AutoCAD command can then be entered in the normal way. Sometimes you may get the error prompt $n>$, where the number n indicates how many left hand brackets remain unclosed. Unbalanced sets of doubles quotes around text strings will also give an error message.

AutoLISP Variables

AutoLISP is one method of manipulating the AutoCAD *variables*. These variables act as named memory boxes into which you can put values. When AutoCAD calls for information of some sort you can automatically feed it the contents of a variable instead of manually entering data.

There are four types of AutoLISP variables: *integer* (whole numbers), *real*, *point* and *string*.

For example: the 'setq' function, written

(setq *variable-name value*)

assigns the specified value to the named variable as shown in the following examples taken from the AutoCAD manual:

(setq k 3)	assigns the integer value of 3 to the variable called k.
(setq x 3.875)	assigns the real number value of 3.875 to the variable called x.
(setq layname 'exterior walls')	assigns the label 'exterior walls' to the variable called layname.
(setq pt (list 3.875,1.23))	assigns the listed x and y coordinates to the point variable called pt.

To use the variable results to answer an AutoCAD prompt you enter an exclamation mark followed by the variable name. For example, when the LINE command prompt asks for a 'from point' then you enter *!pt* as the response. A variable reference cannot be used to issue an AutoCAD command and special techniques are available for this.

AutoLISP functions

AutoLISP has various functions for reading and returning information, and for arithmetic and logical operations on the information. The functions and expressions listed here demonstrate many of the functions while a full set and description is given in the Programmer's Reference.

General

(list x, y, z..)	strings together any number of expressions and gives them as a list.
(setq a x)	assigns the value of x to the variable named a.

Arithmetic expressions

(+ x y)	gives the sum of x and y.

(– x y)	gives the difference of x and y.
(* x y)	gives the product of x and y.
(/ x y)	gives the result of x divided by y.
(max x y)	gives the maximum of x and y.
(min x y)	gives the minimum of x and y.

NOTE: The above functions will operate on more than 2 arguments in the list.

(abs x)	gives the absolute value of x.
(sqrt x)	gives the square root of x.
(expt x p)	gives x to the power of p.
(exp p)	gives e to the power of p.
(log x)	gives the natural log of x.
(flota x)	changes the integer value x to real.
(fix x)	truncates the real value x to integer (e.g.: 2.6 becomes 2; –2.6 becomes –2).
(sin ang)	gives the sine of *ang*, (entered in radians).
(cos ang)	gives the cosine of *ang* (entered in radians).
(atan x)	gives the arc tangent (in radians) of x.
(1+ x)	gives the sum of x and 1.
(1– x)	gives the difference of x and 1.
(angle p1 p2)	gives the angle (in radians) between points p1 and p2.
(distance p1 p2)	gives the distance between points p1 and p2.
(polar p1 and d)	gives the points at distance d from point p1 at a bearing of ang (in radians).
(type a)	gives the type of a as integer, real, list or string.

NOTE: The arithmetic functions simply calculate a result. To change the value of a variable they must be used within the 'setq' function.

String functions

(itoa int)	gives the integer value int, in ASCII.
(atoi s)	gives the integer conversion of string s.
(ascii c)	gives the integer ASCII code for character c.
(chr int)	gives the ASCII character represented by number int.
(strcat s1 s2)	gives the concatenation of strings s1 and s2.
(strlen s)	gives the length of string s.
(terpri)	begins a new line on screen.

Conditional expressions

The 'if' function performs an operation only if some condition is true. There are two forms of the 'if' function:

(if *condition do-if-true*)
(if *condition do-if-true do-if-false*)

The following functions can be used in the 'condition':

(minusp num)	gives t if num is negative, otherwise nil.
(zerop num)	gives t if num is zero, otherwise nil.
(numberp x)	gives t if x is any number, otherwise nil.
(not a b ...)	gives the logical 'not' of a,b,...
(or a b ...)	gives the logical 'or' of a,b,...
(and a b ...)	gives the logical 'and' of a,b,...
(= a b)	gives t if a equals b, otherwise nil.
(/= a b)	gives t if a is not equal to b, otherwise nil.
(> a b)	gives t if a is greater than b, otherwise nil.
(>= a b)	gives t if a is greater than or equal to b, otherwise nil.
(< a b)	gives t if a is less than b, otherwise nil.
(<= a b)	gives t if a is less than or equal to b, otherwise nil.
(listp a)	gives t if a is a list, otherwise nil.
(null a)	gives t if a in nil, otherwise nil.

For example, the expression:

(setq s (if (= 1 0) "Correct" "Error"))

gives the message of either 'Correct' or 'Error' and that result is assigned to the variable s.

Using AutoLISP programs

An AutoLISP program consists of a series of AutoLISP expressions which have been written and saved in an ASCII file with the file type suffix of '.lsp', such as in *window.lsp*. To use an AutoLISP program it must first be loaded at the AutoCAD prompt command line with an entry like

(load"window")

To load a file automatically you should name it *acad.lsp*. When AutoCAD opens a drawing file it will automatically load any file called *acad.lsp*.

Drawing Interchange

The drawings that you create with AutoCAD are normally stored in a compact form of computer file whose filenames have the suffix *.dwg*. These files cannot usually be inspected or modified without the using the normal AutoCAD drawing editor.

It is sometimes useful or necessary to pass the information contained in an AutoCAD drawing for use in another program. Information from other programs can also be usefully imported into an AutoCAD drawing.

This area of drawing interchange is simplest and works best for textual information, such as lists of parts. AutoCAD drawings can also be successfully converted into files for use in desktop publishing programs although full details, such as line thickness, will not necessarily convert well.

The ultimate in drawing interchange is to transfer a drawing file between two CAD packages. Although this interchange is often promised and there are international 'standards', there are great difficulties in transferring full details between two fully featured CAD packages. For example, different CAD packages may use totally different methods of specifying entities, layers, 3-dimensional effects, text and dimensions. It is usually possible to exchange 2-dimensional lines and some other information.

DXF files

The DXF drawing interchange file is AutoCAD's own interchange format which has also become an exchange format recognised by many other packages.

- The **DXFOUT** command generates a drawing interchange file from an existing drawing.

The filename ending '.dxf' is added by default. The DXFOUT subcommands prompt you to select those entities in the drawing which are to be included in the DXF file. The subcommands also prompt you for the decimal places of accuracy.

- The **DXFIN** command generates an AutoCAD drawing from a file which is in an appropriate DXF format.

In order to load a complete DXF file the DXF file must be used in an empty drawing which is free of layers, styles, blocks and other details. If the DXFIN command is used in an empty drawing then only the ENTITIES section of the DXF file is loaded and added to the existing entities.

A DXF Drawing Interchange File is a simple ASCII text file with a filename ending of '.dwg'. The structure of the information contained in this type of file is given in the AutoCAD manual.

IGES files

The IGES Initial Graphics Exchange Standard is an interchange file format intended for exchanging information between CAD packages and between CAD packages and numerically controlled machinery.

- The **IGESOUT** command generates an Initial Graphics Interchange Standard format file from an existing drawing. The filename ending '.igs' is added by default.
- The **IGESIN** command generates an AutoCAD drawing from a file which is in IGES interchange format.

If there is an incompatibility in the file format the input process is halted with an error message, but the partially-loaded drawing is kept.

Index